Steve Jobs
Think Different

First published in Great Britain in 2012 by
PUNCHLINE BOOKS
Suite 7, 40 Craven Street,
London WC2N 5NG

© **PUNCHLINE 2012**

ISBN   9781905382873

Steve Jobs
Think Different

BRANDON HURST

Acknowledgements

Punchline Books would like to thank Andy Hertzfeld for providing us with so much fascinating material about Steve Jobs. Andy worked with Steve on the development of the iconic Macintosh computer in the 1980s. Readers can find out more about those years on his excellent site, www.folklore.org.

'My job is not to be easy on people.
My job is to take these great people
we have and to push them and
make them even better.'

Steve Jobs
February 24, 1955 – October 5, 2011

Introduction

It is human nature to want to put people into boxes. We like to know where we stand; we like to be able to reduce others to a set of narrow impressions or labels. We stereotype them, fitting them into categories that simplify how we can relate to them. The purpose of this is to make the whole messy business of interacting with others more manageable and less threatening, and usually it works well enough.

Steve Jobs defies any such categorisation. He was, by all accounts, a remarkably complicated man. He could be fiercely loyal and loving to those he cared about; conversely, he could be cold, angry, impatient and changeable towards those with whom he had a more ambivalent relationship. He was loved and feared and hated by different people, some of whom did more than one of those, sometimes at the same time. He inspired a mixture of admiration, respect, terror and distaste from his employees and others who knew him well.

Steve's background as an orphan, adopted by a family in Silicon Valley, has been well documented.

So has his personality – one that has been described as 'difficult' at best – and the effects this had on those who worked and lived with him. At least one of his former girlfriends has stated that she believes he suffered from Narcissistic Personality Disorder, a psychological condition that is marked by extreme self-regard, masking a terrible insecurity and a need for control that lies just under the surface and that can lead to outbursts of anger, withdrawal, criticism and rejection of those who challenge them.

Some or all of these fit the Steve's personality, but to reduce him to this diagnosis (accurate or otherwise) is to trivialise someone who did not sit easily in any framework. Andy Hertzfeld, one of his early employees and friends at Apple, remarked, 'Steve was an extremely complex person and I don't think I can rationalize or explain his contradictions.'

This is probably the best approach to understanding the disparate set of characteristics that he embodied. However, it is equally clear that the conflicts which ran through him were a part of what made him – and Apple's products – so great. Asked what drove Steve, Andy did not refer to his friend and colleague's neuroses, adoption or need for acceptance, as others have done. Instead, he says, 'Steve was mainly driven by a passion to do great things – he was extremely passionate about every aspect of the products he worked on and tried incredibly hard to make them transcendently great, sometimes hurting peoples feelings if he felt they got in the way of that.'

Mona Simpson, the sister he did not know he had until he was in his mid-twenties, was in some ways the person he was closest to. In her eulogy at his funeral, she gave some rare insights into what really drove him – some disconnected snippets that shed light on the kind of person he was in her eyes. 'Steve worked at what he loved. He worked really hard. Every day.... He was never embarrassed about working hard, even if the results were failures. If someone as smart as Steve wasn't ashamed to admit trying, maybe I didn't have to be.

What drove him to work so hard was not money or even technological progress for the sake of it: it was something more transcendent. 'Novelty was not Steve's highest value. Beauty was. His philosophy of aesthetics reminds me of a quote that went something like this: "Fashion is what seems beautiful now but looks ugly later; art can be ugly at first but it becomes beautiful later." Steve always aspired to make beautiful later. He was willing to be misunderstood.'

Steve himself was fond of a Wayne Gretzky quote that he said summed up how he thought of himself and his philosophy of developing products: 'I skate to where the puck is going to be, not where it has been.' Comparisons between Steve and other historical characters are many and varied, ranging from Leonardo da Vinci through Thomas Edison to Howard Hughes, to name a few. Whatever the most apt of these, his passion was, as Mona Simpson and Andy Hertzfeld have said, beauty. Andy believes that 'Steve humanized computing, making beautiful, delightful products that were a joy to use and appealed to people's hearts and feelings rather than just practical considerations.'

This biography looks at the broad sweep of Steve's life, with an emphasis on the early years of Apple since this is the period which shaped both the company that came to have such a place in the hearts and minds of so many fans, and on the personality of the man who was so closely associated with it, from its very earliest days of selling the very first machines to 'homebrew' computer enthusiasts. It does not pretend to be authoritative or exhaustive, since these are not words that can be applied to a man who so thoroughly broke the mould as Steve Jobs.

It is tempting to label him as a tortured genius, or some other trite but reductionist phrase that is superficially accurate but ignores the breadth and depth of complexity of a man who transformed first the personal computer industry and then our very culture itself. Steve's contribution to the world cannot be underestimated, and the impact he has had on the way we work, live and relate to each other is profound. Just as the full implications of this legacy cannot fully be understood or simplified, Steve himself defies neat categorisation. Consequently, it seems best simply to tell his story and leave it at that.

1

Steve Jobs was born on February 24, 1955, in San Francisco, to a couple called Joanne Schieble and Abdulfattah 'John' Jandali. Jandali, a Syrian by birth, was a professor of political science at the University of Wisconsin. Joanne was his student, although they were roughly the same age.

Mona Simpson, Steve's biological sister, has spoken about Jandali's background in interviews. 'My father came here from Syria when he was 20, so Arabic was his first language but he spoke to me in English. My Syrian uncles all speak English beautifully. I ate Syrian food as a kid and I've been there and that's about the extent of my cultural identification.'

Steve's upbringing was quite different, and he would find out none of this for many years. He had been born two years before his sister, Mona. Attitudes are very different now, but back in the 1950s an out-of-wedlock birth between a Muslim and an American was considered utterly unacceptable by far more people – including Joanne's parents. The baby was put up for adoption, although the couple later married and had another child, which they kept – Mona. 'They weren't happy. It wasn't that he was Middle-Eastern so much as that he was a Muslim,' Mona said. 'But there are a lot of Arabs in Michigan and Wisconsin. So it's not that unusual.' It was too late for Steve, though.

As a well-educated woman, Joanne insisted that the new parents of her son also had a college education. In the event, he was taken in by a couple called Paul and Clara Jobs who lived in the Bay Area. Paul was a machinist who made components for a laser company, but he had never graduated from high school. Clara was an accountant. Joanne wasn't entirely happy about the placement, and agreed to it only on the grounds that they promised to send her son to college.

Paul and Clara named their new son Steven Paul, and in 1958 they would bring home an adopted sister for Steve, a girl named Patti. When their children were still young they moved to Santa Clara County, California – an area now known as Silicon valley.

Steve's early months were marked by upheaval and transition, and it seems that this shaped the rest of his life. The perceived abandonment at birth is something that some of his closest friends have noted as a key factor in the way that he later interacted with other people – his management style was notoriously abrasive, for instance, and his personal relationships could be chaotic and unpredictable.

It was also a strange time in American history, as Steve himself has observed. He grew up at the watershed between two eras – as evidenced by the circumstances of his own adoption. 'America was sort of at its pinnacle of post World War II prosperity and everything had been fairly straight and narrow from haircuts to culture in every way, and it was just starting to broaden into the 60s where things were going to start expanding out in new directions. Everything was still

14

very successful. Very young. America seemed young and naive in many ways to me, from my memories at that time,' he said in an interview with the Smithsonian Institution.

It would be the better part of thirty years before Steve managed to track down his mother and sister – he effectively remained estranged from his father for the rest of his life, barring all but brief and sporadic email contact. He always thought of Paul and Clara Jobs as his real parents – '1,000 percent', as he said in one interview. He has always considered his father one of his greatest influences and inspirations, and someone who prepared him for his future as a technological guru. 'I was very lucky. My father, Paul, was a pretty remarkable man. He never graduated from high school. He joined the coast guard in World War II and ferried troops around the world for General Patton; and I think he was always getting into trouble and getting busted down to Private. He was a machinist by trade and worked very hard and was kind of a genius with his hands. He had a workbench out in his garage where, when I was about five or six, he sectioned off a little piece of it and said "Steve, this is your workbench now." And he gave me some of his smaller tools and showed me how to use a hammer and saw and how to build things. It really was very good for me. He spent a lot of time with me... teaching me how to build things, how to take things apart, put things back together.'

Nowadays, with the advent and profusion of the integrated circuit, electronics is the preserve of the few, the initiated experts. To most people it is a black box. But back then, electronics was still simple enough for the layperson to access with a little practice and persistence. Steve's father helped him to learn what he needed to in order to give him the confidence to understand and assist in creating some of the first computers. 'He did not have a deep understanding of electronics himself but he'd encountered electronics a lot in automobiles and other things he would fix,' he said of his father. 'He showed me the rudiments of electronics and I got very interested in that. My parents moved from San Francisco to Mountain View when I was five. My dad got transferred and that was right in the heart of Silicon Valley so there were engineers all around. Silicon Valley for the most part at that time was still orchards – apricot orchards and prune orchards – and it was really paradise. I remember the air being crystal clear, where you could see from one end of the valley to the other...'

Steve attended Monta Loma Elementary School but to begin with, he didn't show much interest in education – at least, not in formal education. He had his own interests, and his mother had already taught him to read before he went there. Armed with this skill, he didn't want to conform to the school's own lessons and found its structure suffocating. In fact, he said, rather than foster a spirit of curiosity in him, his teachers very nearly crushed it for good. If they had succeeded, the world might have been a very different place. He became a notorious prankster, constantly getting into trouble with the friends he would hang around with, coming up with new ideas to relieve their boredom. 'By the time I was in third grade, I had a good buddy of mine, Rick Farentino, and the only way we had fun was to create mischief,' he said. One of their best pranks was to gain the combination to everyone's bike lock by individually trading their combination for their friends' ones. 'There was a big bike rack where everybody put their bikes, maybe a hundred bikes in this rack, and we went out one day and put everybody's lock on everybody else's bike and it took them until about ten o'clock that night to get all the bikes sorted out. We set off explosives in teacher's desks. We got kicked out of school a lot...'

Steve was on a bad track, and if it hadn't been for some special people he might have dropped out of education altogether. He didn't have many doubts about where his life would have led if that had happened. 'I'm 100% sure that if it hadn't been for Mrs. Hill in fourth grade and a few others, I would have absolutely have ended up in jail. I could see those tendencies in myself to have a certain energy to do something. It could have been directed at doing something interesting that other people thought was a good idea or doing something interesting that maybe other people didn't like so much.'

The picture he paints is of a boy with an innate energy, a creativity, that had to be channelled somewhere – the only problem was where. The teacher he mentioned, Imogene Hill, had a lot to do with making sure he channelled it in the direction he ultimately did. She was the one who convinced him – literally bribed him with money and candy she provided herself – to focus on his studies. 'She watched me for about two weeks and then approached me. She said "Steven, I'll tell you what. I'll make you a deal. I have this math workbook and if you take it home and finish on your own without any help and you bring it back to me, if you get it 80% right, I will give you five dollars and one of these really big suckers." And I looked at her like "Are you crazy lady?"'

Her strategy worked, and before long she had gained his respect and re-instilled his own desire to learn. Recognising his interest in using his hands, she bought him kits for making simple cameras. 'I ground my own lens and made a camera. It was really quite wonderful. I think I probably learned more academically in that one year than I learned in my life.' When he finished the fourth grade, his test results were so good that his teachers talked about starting him in high school. Fortunately, his parents only allowed him to skip one grade – something Steve was intensely grateful for.

Culture and technology were both moving fast in Steve's childhood. One of the events he remembered happening was the assassination of JFK. 'I remember the exact moment that I heard he had been shot,' he recalled. 'I was walking across the grass at my schoolyard going home at about three in the afternoon when somebody yelled that the President had been shot and killed. I must have been about seven or eight years old, I guess. I also remember very much the Cuban Missile Crisis. I probably didn't sleep for three or four nights because I was afraid that if I went to sleep I wouldn't wake up. I guess I was seven years old at the time and I understood exactly what was going on. I think everybody did. It was really a terror that I will never forget, and it probably never really left. I think that everyone felt it at that time.'

When he skipped a grade, Steve ended up at Crittenden Middle School. It was not a good experience. He was a year younger than the other students, and found it a harsh environment. Bullying was rife, and sometimes the police would have to be called in to control the fights that broke out between gangs of students. He grew to hate the place, which threatened to undo the good work that Imogene Hill had done the previous year. His parents recognised how destructive it was for him, and how bad it would be for his sister. Rather than put their children through that, they moved to Los Altos, and Steve went to Cupertino Junior High.

Steve's interest in electronics had already been ignited by his father and some of the people in their neighbourhood. This was the place that would become known as Silicon Valley, after all, and the government was investing heavily in the technologies that would power the space race and the companies that would underpin some of the biggest developments of the coming years and decades. 'It was really the most wonderful place in the world to grow up. There was a man who moved in down the street, maybe about six or seven houses down the block who was new in the neighborhood with his wife, and it turned out that he was an engineer at Hewlett-Packard and a ham radio operator and really into electronics. What he did to get to know the kids in the block was rather a strange thing: he put out a carbon microphone and a battery and a speaker on his driveway where you could talk into the microphone and your voice would be amplified by the speaker. Kind of strange thing when you move into a neighborhood, but that's what he did...'

'I got to know this man, whose name was Larry Lang, and he taught me a lot of electronics. He was great,' Steve said. One of the things he got into was Heathkits, do-it-yourself electronics kits. 'Heathkits were these products that you would buy in kit form. You actually paid more money for them than if you just went and bought the finished product if it was available. These Heathkits would come with these detailed manuals about how to put this thing together and all the parts would be laid out in a certain way and color-coded.'

This was no mere exercise in paint-by-number, like putting together an airfix model: it was a learning process that provided a foundation for Steve's later work. 'You'd actually build this thing yourself. I would say that this gave one several things. It gave one a understanding of what was inside a finished product and how it worked because it would include a theory of operation but maybe even more importantly it gave one the sense that one could build the things that one saw around oneself in the universe. These things were not mysteries any more. I mean, you looked at a television set you would think that "I haven't built one of those but I could. There's one of those in the Heathkit catalog and I've built two other Heathkits, so I could build that." Things became much more clear that they were the results of human creation not these magical things that just appeared in one's environment that one had no knowledge of their interiors. It gave a tremendous level of self-confidence, that through exploration and learning one could understand seemingly very complex things in one's environment. My childhood was very fortunate in that way.'

At Homestead High School, which he later attended, Steve would enrol in an electronics class and make some like-minded friends. One of these was a boy called Bill Fernandez, who introduced him to a electronics genius named Stephen Wozniak. Five years older than Steve, 'Woz' was able to build things that Steve found utterly incredible. At the age of 19, Woz and Bill were building a computer circuit that they called the Cream Soda Computer, after the beverage they used to drink while they were working on their creation.

Steve was fascinated. Despite the age difference, he and Woz hit it off straight away – thanks in part to Steve's ability to grasp some of the concepts that Woz had trouble communicating to other people. 'Typically, it was really hard for me to explain to people the kind of design stuff I worked on, but Steve got it right away. And I liked him. He was kind of skinny and wiry and full of energy...' As well as the electronics, they also had music and pranks in common. One prank they tried to execute together didn't quite come off: a plan to unveil a giant middle finger on a tie-died sheet at a graduation class. 'Steve got in trouble...' Woz later recounted in his autobiography.

Steve thrived at Homestead, thanks to the friendships and opportunities he met there. One of his teachers has spoken of how he called up Bill Hewlett – the co-founder of the local Hewlett-Packard – to ask him to provide components for his homework. He even managed to get a summer job with the company. HP also ran after-school lectures, which he and his friends would attend. Woz, a huge admirer, would later end up working for the firm.

Steve hadn't lost his rebellious streak, and it almost got him into trouble when he and Woz decided to combine it with their love of electronics in a little money-raising venture. During Woz's time at college in the early 1970s, a new phenomenon was sweeping the nascent hacking community. As phone networks became computerised, hackers started to figure out how they worked. If they were so inclined, they could then exploit its vulnerabilities. These phone hackers were known as 'phreaks'. One of the little devices they came up with were known as 'blue boxes'. These would replicate the tones that the phones used to route long-distance calls, allowing phreaks to circumvent AT&T's switching equipment and thereby allowing free phone calls.

A circuit diagram for one of these blue boxes was published in Esquire magazine late in 1971, and Steve and Woz decided to try making one. To their surprise it worked, and the two of them set about making more and trying to hawk them to the students at Berkeley. They stopped almost immediately, when the police nearly caught them. Woz recounts what happened on his website. 'Once, Steve Jobs and I tried to make our first blue box call ever from a pay phone. This was while I was a student at Berkeley. Steve's car had broken down about 1 AM while driving from Berkeley to his home in Los Altos where my Pinto was parked. We walked to a nearby gas station and were making our blue box call back to the dorms to get Draper to give us a lift. We got very scared when the operator kept coming on the line. We didn't yet have the right operator BS down pat. Then two cops pulled up. Steve's hand, holding the blue box, was shaking. But our looks led the cops to search the bushes for drugs or something. With their backs turned, Steve passed me the blue box and I got it in my jacket pocket.

'The cops then patted us down and found the blue box. We knew we'd been caught. The cops asked what it was and I said "an electronic music synthesizer" and told them that you got tones by pushing the keyboard buttons. The cop asked what the red button (phone line seizing!) was for and Steve said "calibration." The cops were very interested in our blue box. They held on to it and asked us to get in their car while they drove out to our broken down car. We were in the back seat, shaking. Finally, the cop in the passenger seat turned around and handed me the blue box, saying "a guy named Moog beat you to it." Steve responded, saying that Moog had sent us the schematics. The cops actually believed us.'

They had got away with what could have been seen as a serious crime. Having said that, they hadn't exactly been subtle about their enterprise. One legend goes that they placed a long-distance call to the Vatican and asked to speak to the Pope, pretending to be Henry Kissinger.

While he was at Homestead High School, Steve met Chrisann Brennan, his first proper girlfriend. The two of them would go out, on and off, for a number of years, but when Chrisann became pregnant, Steve initially denied point blank that the child was his.

Although this episode was understandably acrimonious, Chrisann was able to remember the Steve she first knew in a piece she wrote for Rolling Stone after his death. Like many of his friends at the time, she remembers a good-natured and relaxed boy who lacked the intensity and burning ambition that so many others later saw in him. 'At 17, Steve had more than a touch of the cool sophistication of a Beat poet,' she stated. 'It is as if Beat poetry laid the future for technology in Steve.' In the tenth grade, he did tell her that he was going to be a millionaire – setting his sights rather low, as it happened.

One story she told from a little later on in their life together illustrates the point of how money wasn't a factor for him. Whatever drove Steve to his successes and failures, wealth wasn't it. 'We had very little money and no foreseeable prospects,' she wrote. 'One evening after we had splurged on dinner and a movie, we walked back to our car to discover a $25 parking ticket. I just turned inside out with despair, but Steve did not seem to care. He had a deep well of patience when it came to discouragements. We drove to the ocean near Crissy Field in San Francisco and walked out onto the beach to see the sunset, where I began talking about money worries. He gave me a long, exasperated look, reached into his pockets and took the few last coins and dollars we had and threw them into the ocean. All of them.'

After high school, Steve decided to go to Reed College – a private, independent liberal arts college in Portland, Oregon. This was a problem for his parents, since the tuition was extremely expensive, but they were obliged to keep their promise to Steve's biological parents and send him to college.

Steve didn't stay there long – at least, not officially. He dropped out after only a term. He found that he could still gain some of the benefits of a college education if he slept on friends' floors and visited the classes that took his fancy. 'After six months, I couldn't see the value in it. I had no idea what I wanted to do with my life and no idea how college was going to help me figure it out. And here I was spending all of the money my parents had saved their entire life. So I decided to drop out and trust that it would all work out OK,' he said. 'It was pretty scary at the time, but looking back it was one of the best decisions I ever made. The minute I dropped out I could stop taking the required classes that didn't interest me, and begin dropping in on the ones that looked interesting.'

Paying his way wasn't easy, though, and these were some of the toughest months of his life. 'It wasn't all romantic. I didn't have a dorm room, so I slept on the floor in friends' rooms, I returned coke bottles for the five cent deposits to buy food with, and I would walk the seven miles across town every Sunday night to get one good meal a week at the Hare Krishna temple. I loved it,' he told the audience at his 2005 commencement speech at Stanford University. In this way he broadened his mind by dipping in and out of whatever caught his eye, without signing up to thousands of dollars of fees and many months of study. It is to this period of his life that he attributes the form of every font on the Mac, and on every computer device he ever made since. 'I decided to take a calligraphy class... I learned about serif and sans-serif typefaces, about varying the amount of space between different letter combinations, about what makes great typography great. It was beautiful, historical, artistically subtle in a way that science can't capture, and I found it fascinating. None of this had even a hope of any practical application in my life. But 10 years later, when we were designing the first Macintosh computer, it all came back to me. And we designed it all into the Mac. It was the first computer with beautiful typography.'

This blend of the technical and aesthetic – and the sheer obsession over detail – is characteristic of Steve's talent. Andy Hertzfeld, one the original architects of the Mac and one of Steve's personal friends, told Top Spot that his contribution was to make the technology accessible: 'Steve humanized computing, making beautiful, delightful products that were a joy to use and appealed to people's hearts and feelings rather than just practical considerations.'

Reed broadened Steve's mind in other ways too. He began to learn about Eastern mysticism, developing some curious ideas and philosophies along the way. He took LSD on a number of occasions, something that he later described as one of the most important experiences of his life. Dan Kottke, one of his closest friends at Reed, was similarly interested in enlightenment and would accompany him on many of both his physical and pharmaceutical journeys. Steve became a strict vegan, and at one point further restricted his diet to only fruit – apparently believing that this would eliminate all mucus from his body, as well as body odour, and therefore the need to shower. (Work colleagues had a very different opinion on this.) He fasted at length, a discipline he continued for many years. Some of his beliefs and practices might have been healthy; others eccentric; others still would prove downright dangerous. There is a school of thought that holds he would not be dead today if he had trusted conventional medicine as soon as his cancer diagnosis was made.

In 1974 Steve found himself short of money, with no real idea of where he was going in life. He managed to gain a job as a technician at Atari, one of the first and most formative video games companies. It was Atari's offerings such as the iconic Pong that helped shape the nascent industry. Its founder, Pong writer Nolan Bushnell, was a hero of Steve's for his unconventional brilliance. Bushnell and Atari would be sources of great inspiration for him when he started Apple. Steve demonstrated some of his characteristic abrasiveness at Atari, though, and along with his habit of not showering this resulted in him being put on the night shift.

This was another formative period for Steve. He would later study Zen Buddhism and at one point seriously considered becoming a monk in Japan. Kobun Chino Otogawa, a Zen priest who had come to San Francisco in 1967 and was another great influence on Steve, convinced him otherwise. Kobun would later be NeXT's spiritual adviser, and would marry Steve and his wife Laurene in 1991. But during his early time at Atari Steve was still intrigued by Indian mysticism. He tried to talk Bushnell into paying for a trip to India to visit an ashram, with partial success; Atari funded him as far as Germany, where they needed him to mend some of their computers. Steve met with his Reed friend Dan Kottke in Germany, and the two of them continued to India.

Their experience was not what they hoped. They encountered extreme poverty that shocked them. Steve gave away his possessions and shaved his head, and travelled to see Hindu gurus. One that they particularly wanted to see, Neem Karoli Baba, had died not long before, and Steve was appalled to find people trying to capitalise on his reputation. He came to a realisation, he later said. 'We weren't going to find a place where we could go for a month to be enlightened. It was one of the first times that I started to realize that maybe Thomas Edison did a lot more to improve the world than Karl Marx and Neem Kairoli Baba put together.'

He returned to Atari, where he continued to impress Bushnell – despite his attitude and personal hygiene, Steve was an excellent technician and was soon promoted. Working nights wasn't too much of a hardship, either. Woz was now working for Hewlett-Packard, and would often visit him at Atari. He loved HP, but on the side he was developing an interest in computer circuitry. With Woz, Steve joined a group of early computer enthusiasts called the Homebrew Computer Club. This would prove a pivotal moment in his life, presenting him with the opportunity he needed to channel his creativity and found the company with which he would forever be associated.

2 | Apple Computer

Both Woz's genius and Steve's ruthlessness are illustrated in one anecdote from those years. The original Pong had been a classic game. It was essentially a simulated round of table tennis, in which two players bounced a ball back and forth across the screen until one of them missed with their 'bat'. Bushnell wanted to develop this into a single-player game called Breakout. Instead of the second player, the bat would be used to destroy a wall of blocks.

In the early days of computer games, even such a simple concept required a complete redesign. Steve was tasked with creating the schematic for the circuit board to build the game on. His pay was to be $750, plus a bonus of $100 for every chip that could be eliminated from the original design. Steve promised to deliver his new version in four days. However, he knew that Woz could do a much better job than him, and convinced his friend to design the board instead. They could then split the proceeds.

Woz worked relentlessly to meet the deadline, finally delivering a design that eliminated no fewer than 50 chips – a bonus of some $5,000. However, Steve had omitted to mention this bit of the deal to his friend. Instead, he paid Woz $375, half of the basic fee, and kept the rest. Woz only found out about this ten years later. He said that, had he known that Steve needed the money so badly, he would have let him keep it anyway.

In the event, Atari couldn't use Woz's design. It was too compact and too complex for their manufacturing processes. The company eventually ended up using a design that employed around 100 chips, instead of Woz's 42. Woz claimed the gameplay was no different on their version, and opined that perhaps they merely hadn't understood his board.

But the Breakout board was just a taste of what Woz could do with a soldering iron. A new phenomenon was moving through Silicon Valley, America and further afield: home computing. Computers had been around a while, but they were out of reach of ordinary mortals. Atari produced video games for bars and arcades, and some businesses used the massive mainframes built by IBM. But there was nothing for the general public – nothing small enough, cheap enough and versatile enough to be of interest or use to individuals. Until now.

Like so many other technological advances, personal computing arose in the Bay Area. Part of that was to do with the scientific opportunities, but part was to do with the counterculture that attracted so many smart and open-minded people – Steve included. 'I do think when people look back on this in a hundred years, they're going to see this as a remarkable time in history. And especially this area, believe it or not. When you think of the innovation that's come out of this area, Silicon Valley and the whole San Francisco Berkeley Bay area, you've got the invention of the integrated circuit, the invention of the microprocessor, the invention of semi-conductor memory, the invention of the modern hard disk drive, the invention of the modern floppy disk drive, the invention of the personal computer, invention of genetic engineering, the invention of object-oriented technology, the invention of graphical user interfaces at PARC, followed by Apple, the invention of networking. All that happened in this bay area. It's incredible,' he told the Smithsonian. To explain why, he added, 'You have to go back a little... I mean this is where the beatnik movement happened in San Francisco. It's a pretty interesting thing. This is where the hippy movement happened. This is the only place in America where Rock 'n' Roll really happened. Right? Most of the bands in this country, Bob Dylan in the 60s, I mean they all came out of here. I think of Joan Baez to Jefferson Airplane to the Grateful Dead. Everything came out of here, Janis Joplin, Jimmy Hendrix, everybody. Why is that? You've also had Stanford and Berkeley, two awesome universities drawing smart people from all over the world and depositing them in this clean, sunny, nice place where there's a whole bunch of other smart people and pretty good food. And at times a lot of drugs and all of that. So they stayed. There's a lot of human capital pouring in. Really smart people. People seem pretty bright here relative to the rest of the country. People seem pretty open-minded. I think it's just a very unique place and it's got a track record to prove it and that tends to attract more people. I give a lot of credit to the universities, probably the most credit of anything to Stanford and Berkeley, UC California.'

Personal computing was a part of that counterculture in its own way. It challenged the ethos of IBM, offering to make computers accessible. The Homebrew Computer Club started meeting in 1975 – initially in one of the members' garage, before moving to an auditorium at the Stanford Linear Accelerator Center. The purpose of the club was to get together with like-minded enthusiasts and trade ideas and circuits to build their own computers. The club still meets today, including some of the original members. Many notable hackers and entrepreneurs started out at the Homebrew Computer Club.

One of the innovations in this area was the Altair 8800, a 1975 design based on the Intel 8080 processor. This was the first time a computer had been produced that was cheap enough and simple enough for enthusiasts to make in any number. Thousands of the design sold in DIY kits, ordered from adverts in electronics magazines. The computer couldn't do much as it stood, though. A second innovation came with Altair BASIC, an interpreter for the computer that would make it more accessible and useful to hobbyists. Altair BASIC was created by Bill Gates and Paul Allen. Bill and Paul recognised that the price of computers was falling rapidly, meaning that exponentially more units would be sold. That meant selling software would also become a viable business very soon. Altair BASIC was the first product for Bill and Paul's new company – then called 'Micro-Soft'

Woz was intrigued by the Altair, and by Bill Gates' BASIC, but he didn't buy one. They were too expensive for him and, thanks to his experience and curiosity, he believed he could build a better one anyway. Keeping his day job at HP, he worked evenings on his pet project. The result was a computer that used a keyboard and regular TV screen, making it comparatively easy to program; the Altair used switches and flashing lights, making its use somewhat arcane without further hardware that allowed the user to connect it to peripherals like a video terminal. Under the terms of his contract with Hewlett-Packard, everything Woz made belonged to the corporation. It was his hope that HP would produce a computer based on his design. Amazingly, though, they weren't interested. Fortunately for Steve's plans, they were swift to sign a legal release, allowing Woz to do what he wanted with his board.

It's hard for anyone who has grown up in the internet age to understand what that time was like. Only a generation ago, computers were still new, an evolving technology that was about to hit critical mass and explode into the mainstream thanks to characters like Steve Jobs and his friend Stephen Wozniak. Personal computing was still the preserve of hobbyists – talented men (predominantly) and women, but hobbyists all the same. It was still possible for major developments to be the work of just a single person: something unthinkable today, in an age of such complexity. Woz created both the hardware and the software, effectively single-handedly building the computer that would later be known as the Apple I.

His friend was impressed with the result, recognising the potential of such a machine, which allowed the user to write their own programmes on it. The guys at the Homebrew club were clearly impressed too, which Steve took as a good sign. He and Woz discussed how they could sell the new computer to the other club members; they could build the boards themselves and let the enthusiasts do the rest. No one else was doing that. He later said, 'There's an old Wayne Gretzky quote that I love. "I skate to where the puck is going to be, not where it has been." And we've always tried to do that at Apple. Since the very very beginning. And we always will.' This was uncharted territory, but Steve knew they were on to something.

Apple was created in 1976. In its early days the company ran out of Steve's garage as they built the boards that Woz had designed. There are various stories why it was called Apple. One was that Steve had been working at an orchard on a hippie commune and suggested the title until they could think of a better one – which they never did. Another story is that it was a reference to Apple Records, the Beatles' label. Still another story claims that they simply wanted to be ahead of Atari in the phone book. Woz himself goes with the first story, though he remembers noting at the time that the overlap with Apple Records was going to cause them legal problems in the future – which it duly did.

Still, at the time, they weren't to know that. They were young, they were just starting out in a brand new industry, they had no money and no assurance that they would succeed. It's clear that, once again, money wasn't the driving factor for Steve. Woz remembers discussing creating the company with his friend. 'Steve had a good argument. We were in his car and he said – and I can remember him saying this like it was yesterday: "Well, even if we lose money, we'll have a company. For once in our lives, we'll have a company." That convinced me. And I was excited to think about us like that. To be two best friends starting a company.'

More than that, building computers was a form of art or self-expression. Steve has often talked about his work as art rather than science or engineering. It seems inconceivable today, when computers are so much associated with the dry and technical, but back then the Homebrew movement was a part of a radical counterculture. 'I think the artistry is in having an insight into what one sees around them. Generally putting things together in a way no one else has before and finding a way to express that to other people who don't have that insight so they can get some of the advantage of that insight that makes them feel a certain way or allows them to do a certain thing,' he told the Smithsonian. 'If you study these people a little bit more what you'll find is that in this particular time, in the 70s and the 80s the best people in computers would have normally been poets and writers and musicians. Almost all of them were musicians. A lot of them were poets on the side. They went into computers because it was so compelling. It was fresh and new. It was a new medium of expression for their creative talents. The feelings and the passion that people put into it were completely indistinguishable from a poet or a painter. Many of the people were introspective, inward people who expressed how they felt about other people or the rest of humanity in general into their work, work that other people would use. People put a lot of love into these products, and a lot of expression of their appreciation came to these things. It's hard to explain.'

Unfortunately, poetry didn't pay the bills and Steve had to sell his only real asset, his VW van, to get started. He raised $1,000 this way, and Woz sold his HP 65 calculator – the first magnetic card-programmable calculator, that initially retailed for $795. One of Steve's Atari co-workers, Ron Wayne, helped them with the paperwork they needed to set up as a company. His reward for doing this was a 10 percent share, whilst Steve and Woz split the remainder between them. The two of them would buy out Wayne within a few weeks for just $800, before they incorporated the company in April 1976.

Steve and Woz enlisted the help of Steve's sister, Patti, and his hippie Reed friend, Dan Kottke. The four of them worked in the Jobs family's garage putting boards together. Right from the start, Apple Computer displayed its characteristic love of a healthy profit margin. The parts for the boards cost around $220, and they would pay Patti and Dan $1 for each board assembled. To begin with, they sold them to a new computer shop – one of the first of its kind, called The Byte Shop – that was opening in the area. They knew the owner, Paul Terrell, from the Homebrew Computer Club. Terrell saw the appeal of the Apple I and placed an order for 50 of the boards at $500 each, so long as they were pre-assembled.

This presented something of a problem, as well as an

opportunity. 50 sets of components for each board represented an outlay of over $10,000, and the newly-founded Apple just couldn't afford to pay that. So Steve took the purchase order for the 50 computers to an electronics distributor called Cramer Electronics and sweet-talked them into giving him the parts on the grounds that he would be able to pay for them after he delivered his completed boards. 'I have this purchase order from the Byte Shop chain of computer stores for 50 of my computers and the payment terms are cash on delivery. If you give me the parts on a net 30-day terms I can build and deliver the computers in that time frame, collect my money from Terrell at the Byte Shop and pay you,' he told them.

It worked, but the four of them had to work frantically to make the boards in time to collect the $25,000 fee and pay Cramer in time. As well as the deal with Terrell, they would make and sell boards on an individual basis. They would sell these for $666.66. There are two reasons for the figure, which has nothing to do with the Mark of the Beast (666). One is that it represents a 33 percent mark-up on the $500 they sold it to Terrell for. The second, Woz said, was that he liked repeating numbers. A handful of these Apple I computers still exist today – perhaps only 40 or 50 in the world. They are widely considered the first real personal computer, and one was recently auctioned by Christie's for somewhere in the region of $200,000.

Woz didn't rest on his laurels with the Apple I. As soon as he had finished it he started on its successor. The Apple II was based on the original model, but had a number of real advantages over it. Woz had managed to halve the number of chips in it but made it run much faster. But more importantly, they made it look like a computer. Whereas the Apple I had simply been a board without a case or a keyboard – enthusiasts would provide these themselves, or else rely on someone like Terrell to box them up for a premium – the Apple II was designed from the outset to be fully-functional. It was not a computer for hobbyists: it was pitched at the mass-market. It came with its own keyboard and case and even had colour output, so long as it was plugged into a colour TV. The graphics were better resolution and BASIC was included, meaning that anyone who knew BASIC would use it straight away.

Steve and Woz had high hopes for the Apple II, but it took a little while to get off the ground. They attended the Personal Computer Festival in Atlantic City in 1976, but the new computer wasn't quite finished yet. Steve and Dan attempted to sell the Apple I but were outclassed by Altair's stall. It was clear from the experience that both style and substance were necessary in this business.

When the Apple II was finished Steve sought to expand the fledgling company, looking for a CEO and key personnel. They also needed funding, which they found in the form of Mike Markkula. Markkula had worked for Intel and retired in his early 30s after making millions from stock options. Along with his business sense, he brought a large slab of cash to Apple: $250,000. $80,000 of this was an equity investment, and $170,000 a loan. He took a one-third share of the company in return. He also brought in Michael Scott ('Scotty'), who would be Apple's first CEO. Markkula would take the helm himself after four years in 1981.

Markkula wanted to use his $250,000 investment to build 1,000 of Woz's new Apple II computers. This was thinking big, but Markkula was well aware of Apple's potential. Unfortunately, this was the stage at which Woz found his loyalties torn: he loved working at Hewlett-

Packard, but the others knew that Apple was going to be a full-time job and more. He couldn't do both. Woz initially refused to leave HP, but Steve later talked him around.

This was one of Steve's greatest talents: he was able to convince people of whatever he needed to. Andy Hertzfeld, one of Apple's early employees, noted this as one of Steve's most powerful traits. 'Steve had many strong talents, but the most important one was his awesome powers of persuasion – he could convince anyone of almost anything, which has obvious practical value,' he told Top Spot. 'He also had an unmatched intuitive judgement of both people and technologies – he was very insightful about which people could really deliver breakthroughs and which were just faking it, or what technologies were worth making risky bets on.' Steve and the others deemed that Woz was instrumental to the success of Apple, and so he had to leave HP behind.

They also needed a new logo. The first one had been designed by Ronald Wayne. It was an olde-worlde-style piece, depicting Isaac Newton sat in thought under an apple tree, with an apple hanging above his head. A scroll around the frame read 'Apple Computer Co.', while a legend on the frame itself read 'Newton… A Mind Forever Voyaging Through Strange Seas of Thought … Alone.' It was singularly unsuitable for a modern tech company, evoking illustration plates from books centuries older. Early in 1977 graphic designer Rob Janoff, from a firm Markkula knew, was brought in to create a new logo: the stripy apple with a bite taken out of it. 'The agency got the account sometime January. The logo was introduced with the new product Apple II in April of that year,' Janoff said. He was left to his own devices for the logo, though his later work for the company had a little more oversight. 'Really there was no brief. But the really funny thing was the only

direction we got from Steve Jobs is: "don't make it cute".
There were briefs on subsequent jobs. First there was the
logo, then there was an introductory ad and a sales brochure
for the upcoming introduction. But it was pretty loose at that
time,' he said in an interview with the CreativeBits website.

Janoff can be credited with creating the Apple logo as we now
know it, as well as the early striped version. 'We presented two
versions of the logo. One with and one without the bite. Just
in case he thought the bite was too cute,' he said. 'Fortunately
he went with the one that gave it the most personality with the
bite. Frankly it was a no-brainer and you would miss the mark
if you don't show some kind of an apple. When I presented
I showed him several variations. Striped version, solid color
version, metallic version. All those with the same shape.'

There are plenty of stories circulating about the bite out
of the apple. The simplest is that it is to distinguish it from
another fruit like a tomato. Other explanations refer to
Adam and Eve, Isaac Newton, even Alan Turing – the so-
called father of computer science. Facing a prison sentence
for homosexuality, Turing is said to have killed himself with
a cyanide-laced apple. The apple with coloured stripes is
sometimes explained as an early gay icon. None of these
explanations are true. 'I designed it with a bite for scale, so
people get that it was an apple not a cherry. Also it was kind
of iconic about taking a bite out of an apple. Something that
everyone can experience. It goes across cultures. If anybody
ever had an apple he probably bit into it and that's what you
get. It was after I designed it, that my creative director told
me: "Well you know, there is a computer term called byte."
And I was like: "You're kidding!" So, it was like perfect, but
it was coincidental that it was also a computer term. At the
time I had to be told everything about basic computer terms.'

The brightly-coloured stripes, Janoff says, had two reasons behind them. One was the hippie culture that had influenced both himself and Steve. 'But the real solid reason for the stripes was that the Apple II was the first home or personal computer that could reproduce images on the monitor in color. So it represents color bars on the screen. Also, it was an attempt to make the logo very accessible to everyone, especially to young people, so that Steve could get them into schools.' Apple have changed Janoff's logo a little over the years, but it is still essentially the same as the ones he presented to the small crew back in 1977.

The new product, publicity and advertising worked. Steve attended the West Coast Computer Faire in April and sold 300 Apple II computers there – more than they had ever sold of the Apple I. It was clear that Apple was going places fast. They sold a total of 2,500 in 1977; two years later that figure had soared to 35,000.

Steve and his colleagues knew that schools could be a huge customer for their computers. The problem was that their management moved slowly. The team knew that generations of kids would pass through school without ever using a computer if they didn't do something to speed things up. 'One of the things that built Apple IIs was schools buying Apple IIs, but even so there was about only 10 percent of the schools that even had one computer in them in 1979,' Steve related. 'I thought if there was just one computer in every school, some of the kids would find it. It will change their life. We saw the rate at which this was happening and the rate at which the school bureaucracies were deciding to buy a computer for the school and it was real slow. We realized that a whole generation of kids was going to go through the school before they even got their first computer so we thought the kids can't wait. We wanted to donate a computer to every school in America.'

That would have been a prohibitively expensive prospect for the new company. 'It turns out that there are about a hundred thousand schools in America, about ten thousand high schools, about ninety thousand K through 8. We couldn't afford that as a company. But we studied the law and it turned out that there was a law already on the books, a national law that said that if you donated a piece of scientific instrumentation or computer to a university for educational and research purposes you can take an extra tax deduction. That basically means you don't make any money, you lose some but you don't lose too much. You lose about ten percent. We thought that if we could apply that law, enhance it a little bit to extend it down to K through 8 and remove the research requirements so it was just educational, then we could give a hundred thousand computers away, one to each school in America, and it would cost our company ten million dollars – which was a lot of money to us at that time, but it was less than a hundred million dollars... We decided that we were willing to do that.'

Changing the law on a national level proved difficult and time consuming, but they were still able to make huge strides forward. 'California thought this was such a good idea they came to us and said "You don't have to do a thing. We're going to pass a bill that says 'Since you operate in the State of California and pay California Tax, we're going to pass this bill that says that if the federal bill doesn't pass, then you get the tax break in California'. You can do it in California, which is ten thousand schools." So we did. We gave away ten thousand computers in the State of California. We got a whole bunch of the software companies to give away software. We trained teachers for free and monitored this thing over the next few years. It was phenomenal. One of my great experiences and one of my biggest regrets was that we really tried to do this on a national level and got so close.'

Apple had hit the ground running, and everyone knew the company had a bright future ahead of it. But in Steve's personal life matters were a little more complex. Just as Apple was really starting to gain momentum, Steve's ex-girlfriend from Homestead High School resurfaced. Chrisann Brennan and Steve had dated sporadically since school. They had broken up several months back and Steve was with someone else. Then Chrisann appeared, pregnant and claiming that the baby was Steve's.

Steve denied that he was the father, though no one else was convinced. It was hard to understand what he was thinking; having been abandoned himself as a baby it was incomprehensible that he would do the same to his own child. Thanks to Apple's success he was now comparatively wealthy, but he left Chrisann and the baby, called Lisa, to exist on welfare. He even swore in court documents that he was 'sterile and infertile, and as a result thereof, did not have the physical capacity to procreate a child.' He later admitted that it was simple denial: 'I wish I had handled it differently. I could not see myself as a father then, so I didn't face up to it.' One of Steve's greatest abilities – positive and negative – was to be able to look past facts that inconveniently didn't match what he wanted to be his reality.

Steve appears to have been a mess of contradictions at this point in his life. None of it made any sense. At the time, Apple had a number of new projects in development, to follow up the success of Apple II. There was the Apple III – an ill-fated successor that Woz had been sceptical about from the start and had washed his hands of (when it was finally released, it bombed). There was the Apple Macintosh, which was started by a man called Jef Raskin who joined Apple in the late 70s. Then there was the project that Steve was working on, the company's main focus of their efforts and hope for the future at the time. The name Steve gave to the new computer? Lisa.

Writing for the New York Times after his death, Maureen Dowd painted a less-than-complimentary picture about Steve and his relationships with women, referring to this episode amongst others. 'His extremes left everyone around him with vertigo. He embraced Zen minimalism and anti-materialism. First, he lived in an unfurnished mansion, then a house so modest that Bill Gates, on a visit, was astonished that the whole Jobs family could fit in it. And Jobs scorned security, often leaving his back door unlocked. Yet his genius was designing alluring products that would create a country of technology addicts. He demanded laser-like focus from employees to create an A.D.D. world.

'He was abandoned by parents who conceived him out of wedlock at 23, and he then abandoned a daughter for many years that he conceived out of wedlock at 23. Chrisann Brennan, the mother of Jobs's oldest child, Lisa, said that being put up for adoption left Jobs "full of broken glass." He very belatedly acknowledged Lisa and their relationship was built on "layers of resentment."'

Dowd mentions an occasion later in life when Lisa believed that Steve wasn't going to pay her tuition for Harvard. Andy Hertzfeld lent her $20,000. 'Jobs paid it back to his friend,' Dowd records, 'but Lisa did not invite him to her Harvard graduation. "The key question about Steve is why he can't control himself at times from being so

reflexively cruel and harmful to some people," Andy
said. "That goes back to being abandoned at birth."'

Perhaps this is a form of explanation, but it isn't an adequate
excuse. Deborah Stapleton, who worked with Steve for
several years in the 90s and who was herself adopted,
wrote in to the NYT after Dowd's article was published.
Her impression of him was similar, though she rejected the
adoption premise. 'He was my client for six years as we
introduced Pixar to the public through an initial public offering
and continued to explain the revolution that was to become
the magic of computer-animated movies. I knew him to be
charming, belligerent, exasperating, logical and wonderful,
all in the same day. But I object to this idea that seems to
be an apologia for his bad behavior: being adopted.

'Andy Hertzfeld, a friend and former Apple engineer, is
quoted in the column as saying: "The key question about
Steve is why he can't control himself at times from being
so reflexively cruel and harmful to some people. That
goes back to being abandoned at birth." To that I say,
"Phooey." There are lots of adopted children out there –
me included – who are able to control our emotions and
do not grow up to be "petulant" brats. Give Steve his
due for all the insanely great things he did, but don't give
him a pass on his bad behavior just for being adopted.'

The adoption undoubtedly played a role in forming his
character, regardless of whether it excused his behaviour. But
the fact remains that his colleagues – even those closest to
him – found him tremendously difficult at times. 'Petulant',
'reflexively cruel', 'belligerent': these describe a man not in
control of his own feelings, not adult in his emotional reactions.
The sense they give is of someone who was literally incapable

of balanced, mature emotion. Rather than assume that this was calculated and intentional – which would make him a sociopath – it makes more sense to understand it in different terms; as if there was a piece missing. It seems that at times, it just didn't occur to him to act another way. Maureen Dowd mentions one other relationship he had in the late 1970s and early 80s, with the singer Joan Baez. Baez was older than Steve, in her 40s at this point. At one stage he thought about proposing to her, but the fact that she was that much older meant that having children was unlikely (making a mockery of his explanation of infertility for why Lisa was not his daughter). Dowd writes, 'When he was dating the much older Joan Baez – enthralled by her relationship with his idol, Bob Dylan – he drove her to a Ralph Lauren store in the Stanford mall to show her a red dress that would be "perfect" for her. But one of the world's richest men merely showed her the dress, even after she told him she "couldn't really afford it," while he bought shirts.'

Steve initially denied that Lisa was his daughter, and also that the Apple Lisa computer was named after her. Instead, a number of different acronyms were claimed, including 'Local Integrated Software Architecture'. It wasn't until years later that he admitted it was indeed named after her.

The Lisa computer took a radical turn at the end of 1978 when Steve and some other members of the company visited Xerox's research centre to see the Xerox Alto. The Alto was effectively a personal computer, although it had been developed for use at Xerox PARC (the Xerox Palo Alto Research Center) rather than for home use. The team were allowed three days of access in return for the option of 100,000 shares in Apple at $10 each, the price they were before the IPO. What Steve found there would forever change the face of personal computing.

Xerox PARC had been set up several years earlier to research new and emerging office technologies, on the grounds that the computer revolution threatened sales of their core product, copy machines. Some of the brightest and best computer scientists worked there and had come up with a number of innovations that would feature heavily in the future of personal computing. Strangely, though, they did not seem overly concerned about keeping these developments to themselves – in fact, it appears that they heavily undervalued their achievements.

The real contribution of the Alto was its 'graphical user interface', or GUI. At the time, computers required users to type commands at the prompt to carry out functions such as load programmes – in fact, to achieve anything. This meant that users had to be computer literate in a way that they do not today. To do anything of real worth they had to know how to use the operating system in some depth. The Alto's GUI allowed tasks to be carried using a mouse and point-and-click execution. Although this is something we take for granted today, 25 years ago it was cutting edge technology.

Steve instantly recognised the power and appeal of the GUI. It democratised computing, taking it out of the realm of enthusiasts and experts and making it available to everyone. You didn't have to know BASIC or any other programming language or command set to open, manipulate and move files and folders: you just had to be able to use a mouse.

Xerox were developing other innovations that impressed and enthused Steve. One of these was object-oriented programming, which he would heavily develop almost a decade later with NeXT. They had also created a small network of computers, an early precursor to the internet.

This would also inform NeXT's computers, and later the iMac. But for now, the GUI was the thing that had grabbed Steve. He decided then and there that this was how all computers would work in the future – starting with the Lisa.

Meanwhile, sales of the Apple II were soaring. Aside from the computer's intrinsic benefits over the competition, its appeal received a huge boost from a programme called VisiCalc, created by Dan Bricklin and Bob Frankston, who had founded a company called Software Arts. Released in 1979, VisiCalc was the first real spreadsheet programme ever sold, and had obvious appeal to businesses and individuals who would otherwise need to carry out their work with pencil and paper. Previously, an error at one stage of a series of calculations had to be corrected all the way down the column, as Bricklin had observed when a professor at Harvard Business School made a mistake on his blackboard model. Bricklin saw that he could automate the process with computer software, which had the potential to speed the user's work many times over. 700,000 copies of VisiCalc sold in six years, and the software was only made available for the Apple II. New and improved versions soon appeared from competitors, but the momentum it gave Apple would carry it through the next few years. Another innovation that helped the Apple II retain its position as America's favourite computer was the floppy disk drive that shipped later models – something that was only possible because Woz had had the foresight to include expansion slots in the computer, against Steve's advice.

Apple's success was phenomenal. They had gone from a standing start – the personal computer market had been practically non-existent before they arrived on the scene – to selling 35,000 Apple II units in 1979. Steve was now a millionaire several times over thanks to the shares he held in the privately-owned company, but it was now time to take Apple public.

Apple's profits were outstanding – the company made revenues of $47 million in 1979, largely thanks to the sales spike provided by VisiCalc. But they had an image problem with Steve. The case with Chrisann and his daughter Lisa looked bad, and the board was worried about the adverse publicity that might come their way if the situation wasn't properly resolved. The date for incorporation was set for December 1980, and they insisted that he put matters right by then. Against his will, Steve paid $20,000 to the State for the welfare they had paid out to Chrisann up to that point.

Back at the beginning of 1980, Steve was still the dishevelled, bearded guy who could care less what he looked like. Author Jeff Goodell got a job at Apple in 1980, and described his friend and colleague in an edition of Rolling Stone many years later. 'I had no idea what computers would amount to,' he wrote. 'And no idea that this guy would turn out to be one of the greatest visionaries of our time. To me, he just seemed like a lost hippie kid.'

That would change over the coming months as Apple sought to court the media ahead of the IPO that December. Steve started appearing in the press more and more often, and needed to start looking the part of the American entrepreneur and face of the computer revolution. New York Times columnist Maureen Dowd records, 'Early on, he scorned deodorant and went barefoot and had a disturbing habit of soaking his feet in the office toilet...' Now, he cleaned up his appearance, shaving off the beard and donning the occasional suit, as well as the signature black turtleneck and jeans for which he was always known in later years. His sister, Mona Simpson, commented at his funeral, 'For an innovator, Steve was remarkably loyal. If he loved a shirt, he'd order 10 or 100 of them. In the Palo Alto house, there are probably enough black cotton turtlenecks for everyone in this church. He didn't favor trends or gimmicks.'

The stakes were raised when the Apple III was released early in 1980, and flopped badly. The computer, about which Woz had expressed concern from the start, had a series of technical problems. Some of these had been caused by Steve's obsession for aesthetic design. For example, he didn't want unsightly vents or noisy fans to cool the processor, but the measures put in place to compensate for this – an isolated power supply and a large heat sink – just weren't sufficient. Disks came out melted, chips dislodged and solder shorted, necessitating a redesign. Thousands of units had to be sent back to the manufacturer.

The Apple II was still selling well – in fact, it remained the company's chief source of revenue for years to come. But they knew they couldn't rely on it forever. Computer design was a fast-moving field, and Apple couldn't afford to tread water. There were too many competitors working to overtake them. That meant Steve's Apple Lisa became even more important. The only other project they had on the horizon was something called the Macintosh, which was headed up by Jef Raskin. Back in 1980 the Macintosh team had just four people working on it. It was very much considered a side-project within the company. Raskin's vision was that the Macintosh (named after his favourite apple) would be a common household appliance, and he said he wanted it to be as 'easy to use as a toaster'. He wrote a memo called 'Computers by the millions'. Although he received permission to work on his vision, it was nearly shelved at several points in its early months and years.

One such occasion happened late in 1980, shortly before Apple was to go public. With the failure of the Apple III to meet expectations, the company realised they would have to change something if they were to retain their competitive edge. A reshuffle was undertaken, creating three divisions. These were Accessories, a department for personal systems which included the best-selling Apple II and the problematic Apple III, and one for professionals and businesses, which included Steve's Lisa. Steve was made chairman of the board, though he had expected to head up his division. This was partly a personality issue – Steve was difficult to work with, and many of its engineers baulked at the idea of being his subordinate – and partly so that Steve could undertake more important publicity work.

The Macintosh team was almost disbanded during the reorganisation. Jef Raskin had to fight hard to gain a stay of execution, and was eventually moved into a separate office building some distance away from the main Apple offices. He had just three months to show the board that his pet project was worth funding.

The company was still going strong on the sales of Apple II, and on December 12 went public. The IPO was the largest since 1956, raising more money than Ford did in that year. The IPO created around 300 millionaires, at which point a number of venture capitalists sold their stakes, vindicating their judgement and multiplying their investments many times over.

The IPO launched Apple into the stratosphere. The publicity campaign and the company's reception by the investing public made for high hopes. But Steve wasn't the only personality problem the company had. Mike 'Scotty' Scott had been brought in as CEO in 1977 by Mike Markkula, the angel investor whose experience and $250,000 had enabled Apple to get off the ground in the first place. As it turned out, Scotty was not a good manager. This was brought home all too clearly two months after the celebrated IPO, in February 1981 – a day that went down in history among Apple employees as 'Black Wednesday'.

Andy Hertzfeld was an employee who joined Apple in August 1979, a few months before the company went public. He records the events of Black Wednesday on Folklore.org, a site dedicated to cataloguing the stories around the early days of Apple and, in particular, the development of the Macintosh in the early 1980s.

'Instead of the normal office buzz, there was a muted sadness hanging in the air. People were standing around, huddled in small groups. I ran into Donn Denman, who had a cubicle near mine, and asked him what was going on. "Didn't you hear? Scotty fired almost half of the Apple II engineering team this morning. He started calling people into his office since around 9am, one at a time, and telling them that they were being fired. I think over thirty people have been fired so far. No one knows why, or who's going to be next. There's going to be a meeting out back around noon when he's supposed to tell us what's going on."'

There was no apparent reason for the firings at this point – Apple II was still driving the company forwards, with excellent sales. Plus, the firings didn't seem to have any sense behind them. It wasn't just 'dead wood' to cut back costs; some key players had gone, including a man called Rick Aurrichio, who was working with Andy on a new operating system for the Apple II.

'Rick was clearly one of the most talented programmers in the Apple II division. He would usually do a week's worth of work in a day or two, and then spend the rest of the week messing around with whatever caught his fancy, usually one of the latest games,' Andy writes. 'I understood how he could be a management challenge, but it made no sense to fire him. He was my partner on the new DOS 4.0 project, which was just getting under way, and the only other programmer besides me that was working on it, so it was especially distressing that they would fire him so abruptly.

'So I joined the ranks of the shell-shocked, and listened numbly to the basement meeting where Scotty explained his rationale. He said that the company had grown much too fast over the last year or so, and had made a few key bad hires, who themselves had hired even worse people. He thought the Apple II division had become too complacent, and that we had lost the start-up hustle that was the basis of our success. He wanted to shake us out of our complacency and prune out the bad hires, so we could start growing again in the right direction.'

Scotty was right about the bad hires – the other execs agreed with him. Steve himself had a term for it: the 'bozo explosion'. The problem, in his mind, was that good people would hire other good people, whereas bad people would hire worse people. But Scotty had gone too far. He'd fired a bunch of people – good and bad – indiscriminately, without even consulting the board. The board duly pushed out Mike Scott, and Mike Markkula stepped into the gap while they looked for another CEO.

Changes were also afoot for Steve. He had been taking a more and more active role in the development of the Lisa, and asked to replace section head John Couch some weeks earlier. But the board believed he was not the best person to be heading up the Lisa project, upon which – apparently – rested the future of their company. They refused. Angry at being denied, Steve instead moved into the tiny Macintosh department, off the main site. From that point on, he always saw the two teams, Macintosh and Lisa, as rivals.

Jef Raskin, the highly-qualified engineer who had formulated the Macintosh project, didn't want to work with Steve. They had never got on, the quiet Raskin finding Steve's abrasive character impossible to deal with. After a few weeks, he complained to the board about Steve. Unfortunately, Raskin was considered reasonable collateral damage to keep Steve happy and away from the Lisa. Steve became the new head of the Macintosh team, and Raskin went on leave of absence, never to return.

3 The Mac years

The change fostered a 'them and us' mentality in Steve that he also sought to instill in his little band of engineers. At the time, the Macintosh was still considered a minor side-project. But to Steve, it became the future of the company. The Macintosh was where it was at. They were the cool ones, the cutting-edge of Apple, whereas the Lisa was a tired remake of the Apple II. The divisions entered into a not-so-friendly rivalry to get their computer to market first. All the passion Steve had was directed into his new baby; the Lisa team received only his contempt for its perceived rejection of him.

Neither was the Apple II where his heart lay any more, for all that it had given the company. Andy Hertzfeld relates how Steve brought him onto his team on Black Wednesday, after losing faith in the company after Scotty's injudicious purge. Scotty had had the decency to ask Andy how he could restore his enthusiasm, and Andy says he had expressed an interest in joining the Macintosh team. 'Lots of people at Apple were afraid of Steve Jobs, because of his spontaneous temper tantrums and his proclivity to tell everyone exactly what he thought, which often wasn't very favorable. But he was always nice to me, although sometimes a bit dismissive, in the few interactions that I had with him. I was excited to be talking with him about working on the Mac. The first thing he said to me when I walked into his office was "Are you any good? We only want really good people working on the Mac, and I'm not sure you're good enough." I told him that yes, I thought that I was pretty good.

'A couple of hours later, around 4:30pm, I was back to work on DOS 4.0 for the Apple II. I was working on low-level code for the system, interrupt handlers and dispatchers, when all of a sudden I notice Steve Jobs peering over the wall of my cubicle. "I've got good news for you," he told me. "You're working on the Mac team now. Come with me and I'll take you over to your new desk."

'"Hey, that's great," I responded. "I just need a day or two to finish up what I'm doing here, and I can start on the Mac on Monday."

'"What are you working on?,' Steve had replied. 'What's more important than working on the Macintosh?"' When his new team-member tried to explain about the operating system he was working on for the Apple II, Steve replied, 'No, you're just wasting your time with that! Who cares about the Apple II? The Apple II will be dead in a few years. Your OS will be obsolete before it's finished. The Macintosh is the future of Apple, and you're going to start on it now!'

As far as Steve was concerned, it was Macintosh vs. the rest of Apple. He hung a pirate flag outside their building, explaining, 'Better be a pirate than join the Navy!'

This must have taken on a certain poignancy for Jef Raskin, who had had his own project pirated from under him. Jef's vision was for an extremely user-friendly, cheap, mass-produced computer that could be sold to millions of Americans. He was the one who had put together the original team, bringing together a small band of men (and one woman) who punched above their weight and possessed formidable collective technical talent. Steve added to this by poaching the members of the Apple II team he respected – including Woz and a man called Rod Holt.

The problem was that the Macintosh was still very much Raskin's project. Steve and Rod decided to change the name to stamp their own identity on it. Over the years, the computer would indeed evolve and change markedly from its founder's vision, but it would always keep the same name. For some reason, they couldn't get anything else to stick. Steve had appeared in Scientific American at the time of the IPO, promoting Apple's products as 'bicycles for the mind', meaning that they improved speed and efficiency in the same way that a bike did for movement. The new name, the two of them announced to the growing Macintosh team, was to be 'Bicycle'. Rod recognised how silly the name was, but it didn't matter. It was only a code-name anyway. All references to Macintosh were to be changed to Bicycle. No one took any notice, and Rod and Steve soon gave up their efforts to update the name.

And so it remained, despite further efforts to the contrary. 'In the Fall of 1982, Apple paid tens of thousands of dollars to a marketing consulting firm to come up with a themed set of names for Lisa and Macintosh,' writes Andy Hertzfeld. 'They came up with lots of ideas, including calling the Mac the "Apple 40" or the "Apple Allegro". After hearing all the suggestions, Steve and the marketing team decided to go with Lisa and Macintosh as the official names. They did manage to reverse engineer an acronym for Lisa, "Local Integrated Systems Architecture," but internally we preferred the recursive "Lisa: Invented Stupid Acronym," or something like that. Macintosh seemed to be acronym proof...'

Raskin might have come up with the original Macintosh idea, but in its final form it was a collaboration of many people. Bill Atkinson's genius resulted in the user interface and graphics software; Burrell Smith came up with the board that made everything else possible. But Andy states that Steve himself was the one who deserved more of the honour than any other one person. 'The Macintosh never would have happened without him, in anything like the form it did. Other individuals are responsible for the actual creative work, but Steve's vision, passion for excellence and sheer strength of will, not to mention his awesome powers of persuasion, drove the team to meet or exceed the impossible standards that we set for ourselves. Steve already gets a lot of credit for being the driving force behind the Macintosh, but in my opinion, it's very well deserved.'

But the Macintosh's success was a long way off. Steve's rivalry with the Lisa group meant that he was pushing hard to get his computer to market as soon as possible. In the spring of 1981, he still expected it to ship in January 1982: an impossibly compressed schedule, given that the team had barely even begun their real work on it. The problem was that no one felt able to tell Steve how wildly unrealistic his timetable was – not that he would have listened, even if they had. 'Steve insists that we're shipping in early 1982, and won't accept answers to the contrary,' one engineer, Bud Tribble, had explained to his team-mates at the time. 'The best way to describe the situation is a term from Star Trek. Steve has a reality distortion field... In his presence, reality is malleable. He can convince anyone of practically anything. It wears off when he's not around, but it makes it hard to have realistic schedules.'

Working with Steve could be both an inspiring and an intensely frustrating business. He had a habit of trashing other people's ideas, but then coming back – exactly a week later, Tribble said – and suggesting it as his own to the very person who had told him in the first place. 'The reality distortion field was a confounding melange of a charismatic rhetorical style, an indomitable will, and an eagerness to bend any fact to fit the purpose at hand,' records the Folklore.org site. 'If one line of argument failed to persuade, he would deftly switch to another. Sometimes, he would throw you off balance by suddenly adopting your position as his own, without acknowledging that he ever thought differently... Amazingly, the reality distortion field seemed to be effective even if you were acutely aware of it, although the effects would fade after Steve departed. We would often discuss potential techniques for grounding it, but after a while most of us gave up, accepting it as a force of nature.'

With a team of such talented engineers on board, it wasn't surprising that the Macintosh project gradually progressed from being a tiny side-show to something that Apple considered of potential importance. It didn't ship in January 1982, or any time that year, as Steve had intended. But the rest of the company did start to open their eyes to the possibility that it might be a viable and important computer after all. This development was a double-edged sword, causing almost as many problems as it did opportunities. The trouble was, once again, Steve himself. He relentlessly talked up the Macintosh throughout the company, with two effects. One was that his infectious enthusiasm caught on, communicating the self-evident strengths of the computer that, not so long ago, had almost been consigned to the scrap heap. The second was that he annoyed people. Anyone not working on the Macintosh team was a bozo whose own product was worthless. And the thing was, the success of the Macintosh was indeed a genuine threat to Apple's other core products. The Apple II was the standard, but it was getting old now. The Macintosh was priced to appeal to the same customers. And then there was the Lisa, a sophisticated office computer. Although it was, in many ways, superior to the Macintosh, there wasn't enough in it to distinguish the two. If the Macintosh succeeded, neither Apple II or the Lisa had much of a future. That made a lot of people nervous – especially on the Lisa team, hence their desire to get the computer to market before Steve could bring his out.

This tension was occasionally aired dramatically, as when the Macintosh team gave a demonstration to about 25 members of the Lisa team in the interests of helping them understand what it was all about. They set up their prototype in the Lisa offices and started to demonstrate some of the computer's programmes and capabilities. Then there was a knock at the door and Rich Page, one of the Lisa's chief engineers, burst in with a furious look on his face. 'You guys don't know what you're doing!' he began. 'The Macintosh is going to destroy the Lisa! The Macintosh is going to ruin Apple!' This was all the more surprising to the gathered staff because Page was a usually calm and laid-back character. Before anyone could reply, he continued with his diagnosis of the underlying problem. 'Steve Jobs wants to destroy Lisa because we wouldn't let him control it,' he said. 'Sure, it's easy to throw a prototype together, but it's hard to ship a real product. You guys don't understand what you're getting into. The Mac can't run Lisa software, the Lisa can't run Mac software. You don't even care. Nobody's going to buy a Lisa because they know the Mac is coming! But you don't care!'

And he had a point. The fact was that Apple's different divisions were in direct competition with each other. They were supposed to be on the same side, but they might as well have been different companies. Although the Macintosh would prove to be insanely popular a few years down the line, the rift threatened the future of the company, risking making the Lisa obsolete before it even went to market – and it was, as Page said, largely down to Steve's inability to manage his frustration at being pushed out of the Lisa team.

Meanwhile, Steve was garnering ever more publicity, thanks to his role in bringing out the iconic Apple II. He appeared on the cover of Time magazine in February 1982, under the legend 'Striking It Rich'. 'America's Risk Takers' read a caption, alongside an Apple computer. The inference was that Steve's entrepreneurship was great for America, and the country needed more like him. He was thrilled that he had made Time's cover ahead of Bill Gates, who would have to wait a couple more years for the honour. It was a great piece for him, and a great boost for his ego, but it also started in motion a series of events that would leave him bitter and disillusioned with the media.

His profile was such that Time considered making him their Man of the Year, and Mike Moritz, who had written the original article, started researching his story. The problem was, the more he looked into Steve's background, the more skeletons he found. He spoke to a number of Steve's close friends and acquaintances, receiving a decidedly mixed picture of the man he had once thought should be a national icon. He also spoke to some people who Steve had crossed in the past – Jef Raskin, amongst others.

The article was duly published. It still featured Steve, but he was not Man of the Year. Instead, the personal computer was designated 'machine of the year'. Moritz published

a piece called 'The Updated Book of Jobs' in Time. It was
a pretty balanced article, which meant that it catalogued
Steve's considerable faults as well as his qualities and stellar
successes. Some of the people Moritz had interviewed
had done so under the condition of anonymity, which
had given them a free hand to say what they wanted.

Moritz's article started with due enthusiasm for the man who
had transformed the field and the local area in which Apple
had taken root. 'His personal worth is on the balmy side of
$210 million. But past the money, and the hype, and the
fairy-tale success, Jobs has been the prime advanceman for
the computer revolution. With his smooth sales pitch and a
blind faith that would have been the envy of the early Christian
martyrs, it is Steven Jobs, more than anyone, who kicked
open the door and let the personal computer move in.'

Then the reality check set in. Steve's expertise as a salesman
was emphasised, but so was what he hadn't contributed
to Apple. '"Steve didn't do one circuit, design or piece of
code," says Wozniak, who was widely regarded as the true
technological wizard in Jobs' corporate Oz. "He's not really
been into computers, and to this day he has never gone
through a computer manual. But it never crossed my mind
to sell computers. It was Steve who said, "Let's hold them
up in the air and sell a few.'"' Another Apple manager
talked of 'technical ignorance he's not willing to admit.'

Moritz catalogued Steve's reputation as a hard task-master,
and quoted a friend on the way that fame and fortune had
changed him. 'Something is happening to Steve that's sad
and not pretty, something related to money and power and
loneliness. He's less sensitive to people's feelings. He runs
over them, snowballs them.' The friend turned out to be

Steve's college mate, Dan Kottke. Steve was so angry that he permanently severed contact with Dan. Jef Raskin commented: 'He would have made an excellent King of France.' Then there was the whole question of Chrisann, and his daughter, Lisa.

Moritz's piece stripped Steve bare, revealing both his greatest strengths and weaknesses. He was depicted as brilliant, eccentric, driven, egomaniacal, disciplined, insecure, inspirational, cruel, visionary, ruthless, open-minded, capricious, decisive, arrogant, determined, manipulative, adaptable and exploitative – all in one article. Steve was furious, adopting a far more cautious attitude to the press from that point on.

One thing the Time article did do was trail the 'Mackintosh', which it called 'a more affordable version of Lisa, priced around $2,000'. At the time the article was published, Lisa itself was only two weeks away from being released: the team had beaten Steve to the punch, after all. But work on the Macintosh was proceeding apace. Steve was driving his team hard, with the core members putting in 90-hour weeks. His vision was firm, his standards sky-high. He brooked no compromise. Just one episode that demonstrates his obsession for aesthetic detail is given by Andy Hertzfeld. A new engineer called Charlie Kellner had recently come onto the Macintosh team, and had figured out how to improve the sound on the computer. The Macintosh's sound capabilities were significantly better than the Apple II's, but they were being held back by the design of the case. Kellner took one of the computers home and figured out what was wrong. The next Monday he triumphantly presented his findings to his colleagues. '"I knew that something wasn't right!", he exclaimed. "The sound is being completely muffled by the case! But I know how to fix it." He had done a series of experiments with the Mac that he had taken home over the weekend, and found that the Macintosh's case was baffling and distorting the sound. He even printed out graphics showing the results of his measurements. Then, after analyzing the data, he drilled a hole about the size of a dime in a strategic place, which caused the measurements to improve dramatically.

'He started demoing his modified prototype, showing how the hole improved the sound quality... The next day, Steve Jobs came by in the afternoon and asked to hear Charlie's demo. He listened to the two Macs, and then decreed "There's not enough improvement! There's no way that we're going to put an ugly hole in the case! Just forget about it!"' Kellner was so disappointed that his 'Eureka!' moment had been rubbished that he transferred back to the Apple II division a fortnight later.

It didn't always go Steve's way, though. Steve had his own icons and they didn't always stroke his ego in the way he wanted. On one occasion, shortly before the launch of the Macintosh, Don Knuth came to give a lunchtime lecture to his team. Knuth was a celebrated professor of computer science at Stanford and someone Steve deeply admired. Perhaps Steve reputation had preceded him too; when Knuth arrived Steve eagerly greeted him, offering his hand and saying, 'It's a pleasure to meet you, Professor Knuth. I've read all of your books.'

'You're full of shit,' Knuth replied.

Lisa launched in January 1983, and as chairman, Steve was present for the launch on the East Coast. Despite the fact that this was supposed to be the Lisa's hour, Steve couldn't resist promoting the Macintosh along the way, telling people that before long a cheaper computer with a better GUI and more sophisticated software would be released. And, indeed, the Lisa was received poorly. People recognised that something superior was coming down the pipeline, and they were put off by Lisa's $10,000 price tag. Plus, none of the Lisa's software would run on the Macintosh. It was an expensive dead-end.

What that meant in practice was that Apple's future rested firmly on Steve and on the Macintosh. Lisa wasn't selling well and the Apple II was six years old. Steve brought all of his persuasive powers to bear in securing the future that had seemed so bright but now looked a lot less secure. A major step in the right direction was bringing on board John Sculley as CEO in April 1983.

Sculley was then president of PepsiCo, and had risen through the ranks to prominence over the years he had worked there. The high point of his career, for which he was still celebrated, was the 'Pepsi Challenge'. At the time, Coke dominated the carbonated drinks market. Sculley's campaign involved offering people samples of Coke and Pepsi, without telling them which was which. The majority chose the drink that was then revealed to be Pepsi. The message was obvious: their allegiance to Coke over Pepsi wasn't based on taste. The campaign became a national advertising phenomenon as Pepsi quickly eroded Coke's seemingly unbeatable market share – eventually overtaking them.

Sculley was a powerful and talented man, and he recognised that Apple could go a long way. He had been head-hunted regularly over the last year by the company, but had always refused. Part of the problem was that he actually found Apple technology confusing; he had an Apple II but was unable to use it. Apple hired a recruiting firm and tried some other big names from tech backgrounds, including IBM, AT&T and NASA, but couldn't tempt them away for one reason or another. They set up yet another meeting with Sculley, who turned up at the Apple offices despite the fact he had already decided to refuse them again.

He had reckoned without Steve, who swept him off on a tour of the company, including the Macintosh. The team had even put together an animation of Pepsi bottle caps moving around the screen. Later they met in New York, where Steve was buying a property. After visiting the highlights and talking at length about the opportunities of the personal computer revolution, Steve finally hooked Sculley with the line that has become immortal: 'Do you want to spend the rest of your life selling sugared water, or do you want a chance to change the world?' Sculley wanted to change the world, and he jumped ship from Pepsi to join Steve's crew of pirates working on the Macintosh – as the new CEO of Apple, that was really all the immediate future had to hold now. His pay was a colossal salary of $2.3 million.

Not that Steve steered the same tiny crew of reprobates from Apple any more. After the Lisa was released, it was all hands on deck to get the Macintosh ready to go, and his team swelled vastly. He didn't let them forget that they were latecomers to the party, displaying his characteristic lack of patience and abrasive attitude to those for whom he had no time. He could be seductively brilliant when he wanted to, but with the Lisa team he did not care. 'I only see B and C players here. All the A players are with me on the Mac team,' he once told them. Neither did the Apple II staff escape his contempt: they were the 'dull and boring' ones.

One of Steve's talents was that he could seemingly persuade anyone of anything he wanted to. As Time recorded in the article Steve had been so incensed by, '"He can con you into believing his dream," says Bill Atkinson, who by some estimates is the most gifted programmer at Apple. A company consultant, Guy Tribble, says that Jobs sets up what he calls "a reality-distortion field. He has the ability to make people around him believe in his perception of reality through a combination of very fast comeback, catch phrases and the occasional very original insight, which he throws in to keep you off balance." By whatever name – the dream, the Ditch, the rap, the reality-distortion field – Jobs' unwavering ambition and ferocious will have caused a number of people to become rich.' But he could turn the charm on and off whenever it suited him. If it served his purposes – as it did with Sculley – he could be the most engaging and convincing person in the world. If someone wasn't of use to him, they were in danger of getting a not-so-polite brush-off.

Journalist Jeffrey Young told the Australian Broadcasting Company about his first – and effectively only – meeting with Steve, a little before the Macintosh shipped in early 1984. 'It was a fascinating meeting. It fits everything that all the stories you've ever heard of Steve, of driven insanity. I was walking through the Bandly building at the Apple headquarters in Cupertino. We'd started a magazine; this is before the Macintosh came out. We'd started a magazine that was going to be about the Macintosh. I was a newspaper reporter in the area and had joined the team as one of the founding editors and Steve caught sight of me inside the Bandly area where I'd been given permission to enter. This was a secret project. He was talking to a couple of other people, stopped in his tracks, put his face in my face and yelled at me, "Who the hell are you?"

'And I told him who I was and he then proceeded to grill me about what my bona fides were, what I'd written, where I'd published, who I was, what I was intending to write. And after about three or so minutes of intense questioning, he lost interest in me completely. Never really engaged with me again even though for six months I spent hours and hours and days inside the Apple headquarters building where the Mac was being developed and I was able to just sort of join the meetings and be part of the whole team. But he never really paid me any more attention because he'd gotten what he wanted, which he'd found out who I was and from then I wasn't moving the Macintosh forward. I was, you know, an outsider, a hanger-on, a journalist, a writer, a reporter. But I wasn't a member of his all-hallowed Macintosh team.'

Getting the Macintosh ready was an all-consuming obsession for Steve. It was a desperate scramble to get everything done in time. Steve's shipping dates had been put back again and again, but now a date had publicly been set: January 24, 1984 – the date of the annual shareholders meeting. There were numerous issues. One of these was the lack of software to run on the new machine – something that would later prove an issue after the release. Apple gave contracts to a number of third party software developers to increase the number of programmes that would be available for the Macintosh, including Lotus and Microsoft.

Bringing Microsoft on board was a short-term strategic decision necessary for the Macintosh to gain early traction, but it opened a can of worms for Steve and Apple. Late in 1983, evidence started to mount that Microsoft were planning to copy the Macintosh. Software developers were asking too many questions; it could have just been curiosity, but sharper minds started to realise that the information could be used to undermine Apple's competitive advantage. Steve got to hear about this possibility, but effectively laughed it off – he didn't rate Microsoft's chances of doing a good enough job.

Then in November 1983, Microsoft announced their intention to release a new interface. Rather than DOS, the command-line prompt system that they had relied on up to this point, they were creating something called 'Windows'. It was to have a graphical user interface, which made use of a mouse and point-and-click functionality to open applications and folders. It was, in other words, suspiciously similar to the GUI that had appeared – to limited effect – on the Lisa and, more importantly, the one that was shortly to take the world by storm on the Macintosh. Steve was furious at this betrayal and demanded to see Bill Gates immediately. 'He needs to explain this, and it better be good. I want him in this room by tomorrow afternoon, or else!'

Thus summoned, Bill appeared in front of Steve the very next day. He alone represented Microsoft, confronted by Steve with ten other Apple engineers in the room. Andy Hertzfeld was one of those present. 'You're ripping us off!' he recalls Steve shouting, his voice rising in fury. 'I trusted you, and now you're stealing from us!'

A lot of people found Steve scary, but Bill must have seen this coming. What Steve perceived as an act of treachery could hardly fail to come to light once Microsoft unveiled their new product. Bill simply stood there, unfazed by Steve's rage, and answered, 'Well, Steve, I think there's more than one way of looking at it. I think it's more like we both had this rich neighbor named Xerox and I broke into his house to steal the TV set and found out that you had already stolen it.'

And he had a point. Apple had, to put it charitably, borrowed the idea of the GUI from Xerox after Steve's visit to their research centre a few years earlier. Microsoft had similarly borrowed it from Apple. Apple could hardly take the moral high ground. Steve barely had a leg to stand on. Indeed, the matter would eventually go to court, and one of the reasons Microsoft wasn't found liable was that Apple had only got the idea from Xerox in the first place.

One of the most infuriating things for Steve was that Microsoft had beaten Apple to it: they announced Windows in November 1983, and the Macintosh wouldn't ship until two months later. This was down to an oversight on Apple's part. When they had first signed up Microsoft to develop software for them in 1981, the contract had specified that they could not release mouse-based software until one year after the Mac shipped. He claimed that Bill was in breach of contract. In fact, he was wrong. The contract had included the old shipping date for the Macintosh of September 1982. As the date was pushed back, the contract had never been amended. Bill had simply been following the letter of the law, doing exactly what his contract specified. There was nothing Steve could do: he needed Microsoft if the Macintosh was going to have anything like enough software to appeal to consumers, so he couldn't throw him out.

The release date inexorably approached, piling the pressure onto Steve and his team of engineers. The core members were used to working 90 hour weeks, but in the final few days before the factory opened – on the 16th January – they stayed in the office 24 hours a day, snatching sleep when they could to give the maximum time to iron out the last glitches in the software.

They weren't the only ones working hard. Apple's publicity department had gone all-out to make the launch a national event, attracting as much press attention as they could. One of the most celebrated and iconic aspects of Macintosh's publicity was the '1984' advert, a 60-second piece directed by Ridley Scott, then famous for Alien and Blade Runner. The concept had been created by advertising agency Chiat-Day, whom Apple had hired to manage their new computer's media perception. The advert was aired in the third quarter of the 1984 Superbowl, where it was seen by millions. Part of its iconic appeal was that it was barely seen anywhere else before or since, until the much later advent of YouTube.

Chiat-Day had actually come up with the idea a couple of years earlier, but had failed to sell it to the computer companies they had approached – including Apple. The short film cost $1.5 million to produce, and was worth every cent. It begins in an Orwellian future, with lines of nondescript clone-like workers filing through futuristic tubes to a central location, clad in identical grey uniforms. A female athlete in red shorts and a white singlet is seen running, carrying a heavy sledgehammer. Shots of storm-troopers mobilising are interspersed with footage of the worker drones sat in their ranks in front of a huge screen, transfixed as Big Brother intones his message of propaganda. The message itself cannot clearly be heard in the commercial, but was actually text lifted directly from 1984: 'My friends, each of you is a single cell in the great body of the State. And today, that great body has purged itself of parasites. We have triumphed over the unprincipled dissemination of facts...' As the storm-troopers close in, the woman bursts into the room and hurls her sledgehammer at the screen, shattering Big Brother's image and ending his speech in an explosion of brilliant white light.

The message was clear to anyone who had read 1984, and plenty of others besides. Apple was the renegade company, the force for good who would smash the stranglehold of the big corporations on the computer market and free the minds of the public. The advert finished with the message, 'On January 24th, Apple Computer will introduce Macintosh. And you'll see why 1984 won't be like "1984".'

The 1984 commercial is another great example of how Steve's instinct proved right, against widespread opinion to the contrary. '1984' was almost pulled. When the concept was first pitched Steve had loved it. He had to work to convince CEO John Sculley to fund it, but managed to secure the money required. He accompanied the Chiat-Day crew to London where the commercial was filmed (using 200 English skinheads as extras, at a price of $125 a day). Young test audiences in America responded well to the first version, and two Superbowl slots were booked for $1 million – the 60-second slot and another 30-second one.

Apple's board was another matter. Sculley later recalled, 'Everyone thought it was the worst commercial they had ever seen.' He instructed Chiat-Day to cancel the two Superbowl slots; Chiat-Day did so for the 30-second spot but said that it was too late to pull out of the first. Sculley faced a dilemma: whether to use another commercial or to take a chance on the ad that Steve loved but everyone else seemed to hate. He chose the latter. It was the right decision: although 1984 aired only once in its own right, it was picked up as a news item by many other broadcasters, resulting in a storm of publicity – for free. Apple's board invited the Chiat-Day team to the official launch of the Macintosh two days later, giving them a standing ovation when they entered the room as an acknowledgement that they should have trusted them and Steve.

1984 captured the Zeitgeist, but George Orwell's estate was quite understandably unhappy about it. It was, after all, a clear infringement of copyright. Orwell's book was still under copyright and will remain so for another 30 years even now. A lawyer for the estate sent a cease-and-desist letter to Lee Clow of Chiat-Day, arguing that the concept had very specifically been lifted from the novel. The use of '1984' in the tagline supported the case that this was more than a vague allusion to an Orwellian society. Chiat-Day and Apple complied with the request and the commercial was never aired by Apple again.

Two days later the Macintosh went on sale, and Steve addressed the meeting of shareholders with an emotional speech. Visibly nervous and clothed in a tailored black suit and bow tie, he began by quoting Bob Dylan's 'The Times They Are A-Changin'. Then he handed over to the board for a business report. In summary, Lisa had done badly but Christmas had been a fantastic time for the latest version of the Apple II. But everyone was impatient. They all knew what was coming.

The consummate showman, Steve's speech had the audience rapt. He had rehearsed it only briefly for the occasion, though had come up with the idea some time earlier to introduce the 1984 ad. Andy Hertzfeld details how he played on the 1984 concept, making it clear that IBM – 'Big Blue', as it is popularly known – was the equivalent of the totalitarian state in the commercial, looking to stamp out all competition with grey mediocrity.

'"It is 1958", he began, speaking slowly and dramatically. "IBM passes up a chance to buy a young fledgling company that has invented a new technology called xerography. Two years later, Xerox was born, and IBM has been kicking themselves ever since." The crowd laughs, as Steve pauses.

'"It is ten years later, the late sixties," he continued, speaking faster now. "Digital Equipment Corporation and others invent the mini-computer. IBM dismisses the mini-computer as too small to do serious computing, and therefore unimportant to their business. DEC grows to be a multi-hundred million dollar company before IBM enters the mini-computer market." Steve pauses again.

'"It is now ten years later, the late seventies. In 1977, Apple Computer, a young fledgling company, on the West Coast, introduces the Apple II, the first personal computer as we know it today. IBM dismisses the personal computer as too small to do serious computing, and therefore unimportant to their business," Steve intoned sarcastically, as the crowd applauds.

'"The early 1980s. 1981 – Apple II has become the world's most popular computer, and Apple has grown to a 300 million dollar corporation, becoming the fastest-growing company in American business history. With over fifty companies vying for a share, IBM enters the personal computer market in November of 1981, with the IBM PC." Steve is speaking very quickly now, picking up momentum.

'"1983. Apple and IBM emerge as the industry's strongest competitors, with each selling approximately one billion dollars worth of personal computers in 1983. The shakeout is in full swing. The first major personal computer firm goes bankrupt, with others teetering on the brink. Total industry losses for 1983 overshadow even the combined profits of Apple and IBM."

'He slows down, speaking emphatically. "It is now 1984. It appears that IBM wants it all. Apple is perceived to be the only hope to offer IBM a run for its money. Dealers, after initially welcoming IBM with open arms, now fear an IBM-dominated and controlled future and are turning back to Apple as the only force who can ensure their future freedom."

'Steve pauses even longer, as the crowd's cheering swells. He has them on the edge of their seats. "IBM wants it all, and is aiming its guns at its last obstacle to industry control, Apple. Will Big Blue dominate the entire computer industry? The entire information age? Was George Orwell right?"' He then carried out a demonstration of the Macintosh, which had been sitting in a canvas bag on the stage all along. The computer even 'spoke' a recorded message to introduce itself.

The audience responded with massive enthusiasm, and the early reviews were generally favourable. Major publications ran detailed articles on the Macintosh. Newsweek had a four-page special. The Los Angeles Times' critic wrote, 'I rarely get excited over a new computer. But Apple's Macintosh, officially introduced last Tuesday, has started a fever in Silicon Valley that's hard not to catch… By the time I got my hands on the little computer and its omni-present mouse, I was hooked. Apple has a winner.'

Expectations for the Macintosh were running high, thanks to Apple's intensive publicity campaign and Steve's boundless enthusiasm for his project. Steve's definition of sales success was somewhat arbitrary: he set the bar as 50,000 computers in the first 100 days. By the time that period finished at the end of April, 72,000 Macintoshes had sold. This was, indeed, stellar success. Another 60,000 sold in June. The future for the iconoclastic company looked bright, and predictions for the summer were even better than the spring.

These were partially realised by high sales of cheap computers to college students. Then came the reality check. In the run-up to Christmas, Apple had expected to sell 75,000 units per month. But by then, the number had dropped to only 20,000. The dated Apple II was still bringing in more than two-thirds of Apple's revenue.

What had happened? One of the problems was the cost of the Macintosh. At $2,495 it was significantly higher than the competition from IBM. It seemed that people were willing to accept the presence of the totalitarian state if the alternative of freedom was more expensive. That wasn't the only issue, though. Due to its GUI the computer was comparatively slow. Plus there wasn't at the time a great deal of software to run on the Macintosh, meaning that customers didn't really know how to use this magical new tool that Steve had described as 'insanely great' at the launch. It was as if there was colossal potential that had not been realised, just out of reach.

Steve's enthusiasm wasn't tempered by the cold water of the sales figures. He didn't seem to realise there was a problem. A further $2.5 million advertising campaign didn't make the necessary difference, but as the year drew to a close Steve's reality distortion field was in overdrive.

In the event, sales would pick up when two other products were released. One was the LaserWriter printer – the first Apple printer and only the fourth laser printer on the market. This initially retailed for $6,995 and shipped in March 1985. Despite its high price it was one of the cheaper alternatives. The other innovation was Pagemaker, which was also released in 1985 for the Apple, and two years later for Microsoft's Windows. Together, this trio would bring about the desktop publishing revolution which would revitalise sales of the Macintosh and reinvigorate a company that had been facing an uncertain future. Desktop publishing was a celebration of individualism, a democratisation of an expensive technology that had previously belonged in the hands of big companies: an early example of the 'i' motif that would pervasively characterise the marketing and ethos of Apple nearly 30 years later. Unfortunately, Steve would not be around to see the sales lift later in 1985.

Whatever the problems in the months following its launch, the Macintosh did indeed ultimately become an iconic product that would change the face of personal computing, just as Steve had predicted it would. Technology site Wired.com published a review of the Mac on Apple's 20-year anniversary, under the headline 'Everything's an Apple now.'

Apple had spent around $80 million and six years on the Macintosh, fulfilling Jef Raskin's original vision of a low-cost, mass-produced computer that was 'as easy to use as a toaster'. It was slated as 'the computer for the rest of us' – the public, rather than scientists and programmers. Instead of complex instructions entered at the command line, it had an interface that a child could use. Early software was targeted to creative users – word-processing and drawing packages. Not only that, but it looked good, too. This was its strength and its weakness; in the early days, many potential customers dismissed it as a toy – something with style but little real substance or practical use.

'But 20 years on, it's obvious the machine has had the most profound impact,' wrote Leander Kahney. 'Although Apple is now a relative minnow in the PC industry, it is fair to say that every personal computer these days is essentially a Macintosh clone, even if it runs Microsoft's Windows. Windows, after all, is the sincerest compliment Microsoft has paid to Apple.

'"It's real easy to see that every computer in the world's a Macintosh," said Steve Wozniak, Apple's co-founder, in an interview with the Baltimore Sun. "There was a time when Windows wasn't Windows. They had Microsoft DOS, and

DOS was lines you had to type… And the funny thing is, when they switched over – Windows 95, Windows 98 – now they've got a Macintosh."' It's hard to deny his point. Even if Xerox had the idea first, Steve was the one who managed to have it adopted as a standard – a trailblazer who influenced practically every computer interface created ever since.

The Mac's GUI was 10 years ahead of the competition at the time. Even now, 'The company's products are still a couple of years ahead of the rest of the industry, and in many ways set the standards that all the others adopt. If Apple embraces a technology, the industry usually follows suit down the line. Examples abound – the graphical user interface, Ethernet, USB, WiFi and Bluetooth, which hasn't taken off yet, but will...' Kahney continued in 2004.

Jef Raskin was able to look beyond his dismissal and Steve's acquisition of the project that had been his 25 years earlier, and commented on how the Mac had changed the industry forever. 'It inaugurated a fundamental change in the way we use personal computers, and popularized and improved on the GUI paradigm. Windows, awkward though it be to use, further propagated ideas first seen on the Mac (some of which were available still earlier at Xerox). At first the GUI was a great advance over what came before, but the initial simplicity has been lost and now you have to have a good deal of arcane and "inside" information to use a GUI effectively – or be able to call on a friend for help.

'The ease of use that the Mac introduced made it possible for millions of people to use the next and more important development: a multitude of applications. And then – most important of all – came the Internet and the Web. The use of computers as computers, that is, as user-programmable devices, has almost disappeared. They have become, to use my own coinage, information appliances. In 1979, I specified a long list that covered most of the things we would do with it though I missed four major uses: gambling, pornography, sending spam and spreading viruses.'

Further programmes would soon increase the appeal of the Macintosh, making it more of the 'bicycle for the mind' that Steve had hoped. Much of that software would be developed by Microsoft. Unfortunately, Apple's oversight with the contract in their relationship with Microsoft meant that they were storing up problems for the future. Bill Gates would soon be able to use the same programmes – including Microsoft Word – on Windows, undermining Apple's advantage.

But the problems that would arise from that oversight would take many years to unwind and reach a head. Apple had more serious problems in the short term. One was the lacklustre sales of the Macintosh. Steve had enthusiastically predicted the company would ship two million units by 1985. The reality was just 250,000. After a stellar start, they were reduced to relying on the Apple II to make ends meet.

4 | What NeXT?

Coupled with Steve's management style, his denial of the Mac's trouble in the marketplace was a serious issue. It wasn't just the employees; even the board found him difficult to work with, and had to take difficult steps to manage him. Andy Hertzfeld mentions an incident that captures how some of them felt about him. 'One day Apple executive Jean-Louis Gassee, who had recently transferred to Cupertino from Paris, had just parked his car and was walking toward the entrance of the main office at Apple when Steve buzzed by him in his silver Mercedes and pulled into the handicapped space near the front of the building. As Steve walked brusquely past him, Jean-Louis was heard to declare, to no one in particular, "Oh, I never realized that those spaces were for the emotionally handicapped..."' Some of the people he regularly interacted with started to wonder whether there was something more significant lying behind his unpredictable manner, such as a mild form of bipolar disorder. Maureen Dowd notes one writers comparison of Steve to Shakespeare's Henry V: a 'callous but sentimental, inspiring but flawed king.' 'There were Rasputin-like seductions followed by raging tirades. Everyone was either a hero or bozo,' she summarised.

CEO John Sculley was starting to have particular problems

with him. The early days of their relationship had gone well, from a slightly awkward start to a strong friendship and close collaboration. Sculley was a very different man to Steve, having come from a strict and driven background. Steve seemed to have an easy charisma that he could turn on and off, depending on what suited him; Sculley, on the other hand, had to work at interacting and found it daunting every time. He had managed to overcome a childhood stutter and shyness through sheer effort and determination – the same qualities that won him superb grades and the captaincy of the school football team. Knowing that public speaking was a skill he had to master, he says he watched dozens of movies, learning how famous actors engaged with their audiences in their tone and body language. In front of the press, Sculley was charismatic and inspirational.

It seemed like an unlikely alliance, but he and Steve hit it off. It probably helped that Sculley took a back seat while he found his feet, meaning that Steve and the other execs were more-or-less free to do as they chose while he learned about the company inside out; although marketing was his forté, he didn't have the technical background some of the others thought was important for a computer company. Consequently, he had left the Macintosh project alone, allowing Steve to rule it as he wished. Sculley didn't even have much to do with the marketing campaign, as evidenced by Steve's freedom to run with 1984, despite the fact that Sculley thought it would be a disaster. Their relationship extended outside of work, with the two hiking in the mountains in the surrounding area. It was a good alliance. 'Apple has one leader, Steve and me,' Sculley once said.

After the Mac's launch, that relationship started to stall. (In fairness, one part of the reason for its failure was the price tag, and it had been Sculley's idea to set it at $2,495 – a profit margin of 55 percent. Even by Apple's standards, this was high.) Apple II sales were falling now, and the Macintosh wasn't filling the gap. Steve's enthusiasm and resistance to challenge meant that the official sales forecasts were still in the region of 75,000, despite the fact that they were really selling about a quarter of that. Sales teams knew what was really going on, but no one had had the courage to change the official predictions. Sculley soon felt the tension between his professional and personal relationship with Steve. He needed Steve to take care of the sales and technical issues, but Steve took his ideas increasingly personally, as if they were attacks on his competence. Steve became harder and harder to work with, for his engineers as well as the CEO. Complaints about him increased at every level of the company.

Apple's board was slowly coming around to the idea that Steve wasn't the solution to the Macintosh's problems: he was one of the causes. Sculley's suggestions to Steve were met with hostility, and the glowing future that they had looked forward to together only months earlier now appeared to be receding into the distance. When Microsoft partnered with IBM – an option Sculley had presented to Steve as a way to improve the Macintosh's prospects, but that Steve had vetoed – everyone knew something had to be done. There was enough competition arising in the personal computer market without Steve hamstringing their chances of keeping the edge they'd had with Apple II.

At the time, Steve was working on the Mac's follow-up, the BigMac. The BigMac was supposed to be the answer to a growing demand that Steve had first encountered in 1983 on a trip to the computer lab at Brown University. There he heard about the need for a '3M' machine: one that had a megabyte of memory, a million-pixel display, and a megaflop of processing power. (Steve didn't know what a megaflop – one million floating-point operations per second – was at the time, but had nevertheless stated his belief in the need for such a machine and that Apple would come up with it before anyone else.) That was what was felt necessary as an effective education computer at the time. The Macintosh wasn't even close – it was out by an order of magnitude in each of those requirements.

Steve had Apple buy an expensive Unix licence to provide the foundation for the new and powerful operating system. But the project was beset with technical issues and never got off the ground, although some of its innovations later made it into the Mac II. Millions of dollars later, Apple's board had to admit that the BigMac was a dead end. It was clear that far from being the company's biggest asset, as he had arguably once been, he was now a serious liability. That fact put him in direct conflict with Sculley. The board hoped that Steve could be talked into a sideways move out of a product development role – it was clear he wasn't suited to managing the technical or personal side of things. But Steve fought back and argued that it was Sculley who should go. Long meetings followed, and in April 1985 Sculley received approval to have the Macintosh division reshuffled. Steve would still be Apple's chairman, but would have no clear and active role any more.

He hesitated in actually implementing this momentous development because he wanted to give Steve time to come around to the idea. After all, Steve was – or at least had been – a close friend, and had considerable talent to offer Apple. It was just that he wasn't an asset where he was.

Steve used the time to organise a board-room coup. The plan was to have the board boot him out while Sculley was away on a forthcoming trip to China to talk about education and personal computers. He spoke to the different execs, feeling out what support there might be for his move. The last person he approached was Jean-Louis Gassée, who had worked for Hewlett-Packard before coming in as head of Apple France in 1981. Gassée had never liked Steve and immediately informed Sculley, who cancelled his trip and called an emergency meeting.

A fierce confrontation ensued. Sculley was horrified about the underhand way Steve had gone about trying to have him pushed out. Steve, in return, was forthright about what he saw as the problem. 'I think you're bad for Apple and I think you're the wrong person to run this company,' he told his one-time friend. Sculley responded by asking each member of the board to choose between him and Steve. The board sided with Sculley. All of Steve's responsibilities were cancelled and he was moved out of the main offices into a separate building so remote from the Apple headquarters that he termed it 'Siberia'.

News of the effective demotion was released at the end of May. It coincided with results showing a loss for that quarter for the first time in Apple's existence. Over the next few months, while Steve was still chairman but toothless, he had plenty of time to think about what his next move would be. He travelled extensively, trying to figure out what had gone wrong.

There were plenty of suggestions along the way. In August, Fortune magazine put him on its cover. Instead of the glowing, or at least mixed, pieces he was used to, the story was titled: 'The Fall of Steve Jobs: Behind the Scenes at Apple Computer.' It catalogued what had gone wrong between him and Sculley.

Eventually, he resigned. Apple's stock actually rose $1 as a result, vindicating the board's decision to sideline him. It was scant good news; shares were trading around the $17 mark, down from a high of $64 two years earlier. Although the final move was Steve's choice, there was no doubt that he had been ousted. He had been pushed from the very company he had founded. Time – hardly his greatest friend after the Moritz piece detailing his character flaws as well as his business triumphs – ran a piece called 'Shaken to the Very Core', detailing some of the events that had led to this pass. 'While relations between Jobs and Sculley have been strained at least since last spring, the final rift erupted in a matter of days. On Sept. 12, Jobs informed Apple's board that he was planning to start a new firm; he implied that he would not take any key Apple employees with him. But the brief era of good feeling that ensued lasted less than a day. Just before the start of a 7:30 meeting the following morning, Jobs handed Sculley a letter stating that several major Apple players were leaving to work for his new company. Apple executives could not contain their ire, shouting "liar" and "deceitful" during the meeting. The outcry convinced Jobs that he could no longer stay at the company.

'In a characteristically petulant move, the chairman leaked his letter of resignation to the press hours before delivering it to Apple on Sept. 17. "The company's recent reorganization," Jobs wrote, "has left me with no work to do and no access even to regular management reports. I am but 30, and want still to contribute and achieve." Apparently intended to arouse sympathy, the tone of the letter and its public release struck some Apple executives as a clear attempt to embarrass them. Said Steve Wozniak, Apple's co-founder who left the company last February to establish his own electronics firm: "Steve can be an insulting and hurtful guy." One wag dubbed Jobs the John McEnroe of business.'

83

If it was embarrassing to Apple's board, it was worse for Steve. 'At 30 I was out. And very publicly out,' he said of that time, many years later. 'What had been the focus of my entire adult life was gone, and it was devastating. I really didn't know what to do for a few months. I felt that I had let the previous generation of entrepreneurs down – that I had dropped the baton as it was being passed to me. I met with David Packard and Bob Noyce and tried to apologize for screwing up so badly. I was a very public failure, and I even thought about running away from the Valley.' He wrote to Mike Markkula, stating how the series of events had left him emotionally stunned. 'I feel like somebody just punched me in the stomach and knocked all my wind out. I'm only 30 years old and I want to have a chance to continue creating things. I know I've got at least one more great computer in me. And Apple is not going to give me a chance to do that.'

Meanwhile, Sculley had thrown himself into trying to rescue Apple. The company was a mess, with lack of communication between engineers and marketers meaning that different parts of the company were effectively competing against each other for the same customers. That had been one of the problems with Lisa: Steve's enthusiasm for the Macintosh had turned another one of the company's core projects into a white elephant.

Sculley undertook a restructure, bringing all of the development activities together into one department so that there could never be the kind of intra-company competition that had nearly killed Apple. There would be separate manufacture and marketing departments, with the heads all reporting directly to Sculley. It was a far more orthodox structure; one of Apple's problems was that it had grown somewhat organically, leading to needless complexity and inefficiency.

Sculley's foresight and courage to make the necessary changes reaped huge rewards. By 1989, Mac sales would top three million – ten times more than in 1985. The new management team had a more hands-off style, allowing engineers to follow their instincts and be as creative as they liked. Apple turned a corner, but the more conventional structure also sowed the seeds of stagnation, the company becoming a staid and bureaucratic institution rather than the cool trend-setter that had wowed audiences with '1984'. Mismanagement and poor hiring choices would result in millions of dollars being thrown into bottomless research pits that could never realistically have delivered, like Apple's attempt to build its own chips. Maybe Steve saw some of this, with quiet satisfaction. But at this point, that time was still a decade away.

Steve's sister, Mona Simpson, would later speak of how hard this time was for him. 'When he got kicked out of Apple, things were painful. He told me about a dinner at which 500 Silicon Valley leaders met the then-sitting president. Steve hadn't been invited. He was hurt but he still went to work at NeXT. Every single day.' The board-room coup was one of the most painful experiences of Steve's life but, with hindsight, he says it was also one of the best. It released him from Apple to enjoy the creative freedom that he could not exercise if he had stayed.

Steve was intrigued by the idea of an affordable 3M computer, something that seemed so far out of reach when he had first heard about it. At least a couple of experiences during his time in the wilderness had convinced him that the concept had real mileage in it. In that period of exile from Apple in Siberia, he had chanced across Industrial Light and Magic, a division of LucasArts. ILM had a vision for CGI a clear decade before its use became mainstream. Computers weren't up to the job at the time, but they knew that once they were then remarkable developments might come in film. George Lucas didn't share their passion and was trying to sell the division.

Then there was Paul Berg, who was carrying out research into DNA at Stanford University. Berg had met with Steve and asked him whether there was a computer available that could be used to model the complex molecules he worked with. It seemed that, from various quarters, there was demand for a 3M computer.

Steve might have been down, but he wasn't out. On paper, he was a multi-millionaire, thanks to the stock he held in Apple. He had more than enough money to start a new venture. When he left, he also took with him a number of key personnel from Apple, including some of the people whose expertise had been central in getting the Mac off the ground. That, and the clear competition with the beleaguered BigMac project, led to the acrimonious split that resulted in a lawsuit.

Steve's new company was called NeXT. The idea was to create a high-end computer for educational use. The out-of-court settlement with Apple initially hobbled them in terms of product development, but Steve set about doing things properly from the start. He wanted to create a close-knit fraternity of people. There was huge hype around NeXT, with highly-qualified engineers clamouring for a piece of the action. It was big news in Silicon Valley. Despite Steve's ignominious departure from Apple, expectations were sky-high. He was still a legend. News also spread of the ethos of his new company. He poured his own money into NeXT, ensuring that the work environment was anything but corporate. To begin with, there were only two pay grades: senior staff received a salary of $75,000 and everyone else received $50,000.

There were numerous bonuses – gym membership, financial assistance, counselling and other little touches that meant staff felt cared about, not exploited. For someone who could rub people up the wrong way so badly, Steve's attention to detail in the interests of keeping staff happy was remarkable.

Around this time, Steve met a computer consultant called Tina Redse, a tall blonde woman with whom he fell in love. Like everything in his life, Steve did relationships to extremes; he once said that she was the first woman he really loved, and their time together was intense, marked with highs and lows of 'intense passion and severe emotional detachment', as one writer described it. They lived together for some years, but the relationship was never stable; there would be unpleasant fights, after one of which she wrote on their apartment wall, 'neglect is a form of abuse'. In 1989 Steve asked Tina to marry him, but she turned him down – which would prove to be the end of the relationship. She later said that she believed he suffered from narcissistic personality disorder, a mental condition characterised by a high degree of self-centredness, masking extreme insecurity. Those with narcissistic personality disorder have a certain self-image and are very hard to challenge, often flying into rages when someone does something that is perceived as an attack. They tend to micromanage and manipulate to get whatever they want; they can be extremely charming when it is in their interests, but cold, unkind and disinterested at other times. Tina Redse isn't the only person to have thought that he perfectly met the psychological criteria for the condition. 'Expecting him to be nicer or less self-centered was like expecting a blind man to see,' she said.

There were other big changes afoot in Steve's personal life. He had started looking for his biological mother with the help of a private detective, and finally managed to track her down. She told him that he also had a sister, the novelist Mona Simpson. It transpired that Joanne Schieble, Steve's mother, had ultimately married Abdulfattah 'John' Jandali, not long after they had given their son up for adoption. Joanne's father had been against the marriage, threatening to disown her if they went ahead. However, he had died not long afterwards and the two had married. Joanne had given birth to Mona, but five years later Jandali had left them.

In her eulogy at his funeral, Mona described the experience of learning who her brother was. 'By then, I lived in New York, where I was trying to write my first novel. I had a job at a small magazine in an office the size of a closet, with three other aspiring writers. When one day a lawyer called me – me, the middle-class girl from California who hassled the boss to buy us health insurance – and said his client was rich and famous and was my long-lost brother, the young editors went wild. This was 1985 and we worked at a cutting-edge literary magazine, but I'd fallen into the plot of a Dickens novel and really, we all loved those best. The lawyer refused to tell me my brother's name and my colleagues started a betting pool. The leading candidate: John Travolta. I secretly hoped for a literary descendant of Henry James – someone more talented than I, someone brilliant without even trying.'

Steve was also thrilled that he was related to a woman who would become an award-winning novelist, another creative type like him, and he displayed her book, Anywhere But Here, at the NeXT offices. Ten years later, she would pen A Regular Guy. The novel is heavily influenced by these years of her life, to the point where many insights into Steve's life can be gained by reading it. Its protagonist, Tom Owens, drops out of college to invent 'a new kind of business' in Silicon Valley. His efforts are disturbed when a young daughter born out of wedlock turns up out of the blue.

There is no question that Steve and Mona grew close. In her eulogy, Mona recalled that her hopes about her father were consistently disappointed, but that she found something of what she had been looking for in Steve. 'I grew up as an only child, with a single mother. Because we were poor and because I knew my father had emigrated from Syria, I imagined he looked like Omar Sharif. I hoped he would be rich and kind and would come into our lives (and our not yet furnished apartment) and help us. Later, after I'd met my father, I tried to believe he'd changed his number and left no forwarding address because he was an idealistic revolutionary, plotting a new world for the Arab people. Even as a feminist, my whole life I'd been waiting for a man to love, who could love me. For decades, I'd thought that man would be my father. When I was 25, I met that man and he was my brother.'

Steve's own daughter, Lisa, was starting to play a greater role in his life at this point, and it is not hard to see the parallels. She spent more time with him, both at his home and the NeXT offices, and he started to take more of an active interest in her life and education.

Mona decided to find her father, Jandali, but Steve wasn't interested. He would later claim that he held nothing against the man, who he sometimes described simply as a 'sperm donor'. He said that what put him off the most was that 'he didn't treat Mona well. He abandoned her.' Steve can hardly take the moral high ground here, having effectively treated his own daughter the same way for several years. His motivations were clearly complex, with denial, fear and insecurity playing a large part. It is probable that there was more to it than that, and that his reluctance to see Jandali also came from such a place. How would it be to confront a man who had decided he didn't want his son? For someone like Steve, whose ego was so fragile, that might prove too much. It seems likely that his dismissal of Jandali on the grounds that he treated Mona badly was partly projection, attributing the feelings he found so unacceptable in himself to another person.

In the sort of twist of fate that usually only occurs in movies, it appears that Steve and his biological father really did meet on at least one occasion, but did not know it at the time. Mona had hired a private detective who had tracked Jandali down to a restaurant in Sacramento, where he worked. The detective reported that Jandali had said he had had another child with Joanne, before they were married. He said that the baby was gone, and that they would never see him again. In the same conversation, however, he had talked about another restaurant he had managed, not far from the Apple offices. He mentioned that a lot of big names from Silicon Valley used to eat there – including Steve Jobs, who he described as a 'sweet guy and a big tipper.'

Steve, too, remembered meeting him. Mona told him about Jandali and he recalled a 'balding Syrian' with whom he had once shaken hands. However, he had no intention of learning more, and asked his sister not to tell Jandali who he was. It seems that in later years they may have had some very limited contact, but nothing of any real significance. Steve was very rich by then, and didn't want Jandali exacting money from him by blackmail, or going to the press.

NeXT was struggling getting its new 3M computer off the ground, and Steve was throwing his own money at the company. Late in 1986, a documentary was broadcast on CBS that would change that. It was called The Entrepreneurs and featured Steve and his new company and employees. It was seen by a man called Ross Perot, a man who had made his millions in the tech industry. He had owned a company, Electronic Data Systems, that provided trained data-handlers along with computer hardware. In 1984 he had sold it to General Motors for $2.5 billion. He was captivated with what NeXT was trying to do and offered investment capital to Steve. Perot took a 16 percent share of NeXT for a sum of $20 million, despite the fact that it then had no products to speak of. This was a testament to the clout that Steve still had in Silicon Valley, even after his fall from Apple.

There were plenty of things to spend Perot's money on. NeXT needed a logo and a brand; Steve asked around for 'the best logo designer on the planet' and was given the name Paul Rand. Rand was a graphic designer who had gained prominence for his corporate logos, amongst other things. In 1981 he had created the 'Eye Bee M' logo for IBM. For the fee of $100,000 he produced NeXT's new logo, including the lower-case 'e' – signifying 'education, excellence, expertise, exceptional, excitement, e=mc2...' In other words, all things aspirational. Steve also hired an interior designer and had him decorate their premises in the Stanford Industrial Park, one of Silicon Valley's most expensive areas. These were furnished with huge sofas, hardwood floors and Ansel Adams prints.

Steve wanted to ensure that his products were just as beautifully and carefully designed, with an obsessive eye for detail. Their hardware, software and aesthetics were all cutting edge. Manufacture would be computer-controlled and set up for mass-production. He bought a Unix licence, as he had got Apple to do for the now-defunct BigMac project, in order to build a new and powerful operating system. He had his engineers give it a GUI, as with every product he had worked on since Lisa, in order to make it accessible to the mass-market. He also took a punt on an emerging technology; instead of giving the machine a floppy disk drive (which Steve hated) he bet on magneto-optical drives. This was, again, ahead of its time, although the iMac would later be the first successful computer to do away with floppy disks altogether.

It was indeed a visionary project, but also a huge undertaking that required a lengthy period of development. It suffered delay after delay, but was finally unveiled to great fanfare in October 1988. The NeXT factory was set in motion and the computer he had spent three years overseeing, the NeXT Computer, hit the market in 1988. It was informally known as the Cube, since it was housed in a one-foot cubic die-cast magnesium box.

Steve was a great showman and the launch of the NeXT Computer was a major event, with audiences rapt with attention at this new 3M machine. However, the smooth sales pitch glossed over a number of problems with the computer. Not the least of these was its price. At $6,500, the Cube was too expensive for many of the universities for which it had been designed in the first place. They had expected to pay less than half that for the machine they needed. There were other problems. Many users would require a hard disk (at a price of a further $3,000) because the magneto-optical drive was so slow it made it almost unusable. Neither was the operating system, NeXTSTEP, ready – the finished version would take another six months. It was a revolutionary machine, and the first on the market of its type, but the fact remained that few people or institutions had the money to buy one.

The NeXT factory was capable of rolling 10,000 computers off its production lines every month, but in 1989 it averaged only 400 per month. There simply wasn't the demand. NeXT continued to devour cash, its biggest assets failing to recoup the huge investments made in them.

Meanwhile at Apple, things were looking up a little thanks to improving sales, but the long-term picture didn't seem great. The company had reached a legal settlement with Steve, allowing them to wash their hands of him and Steve to create the NeXT Computer. In return, Steve had to agree not to poach any more Apple employees for at least six months. Apple engineers were given access to the NeXT system to ensure that it did not rely on their technology.

There was obviously still a great deal of tension between the Apple board and Steve, though CEO John Sculley tried to cover over this in the press. 'I would obviously like to see the time come when Steve Jobs can be as welcome at Apple Computer as Steve Wozniak is,' he said, just before the settlement was made. Woz, who had been such a key player at Apple, had left in 1985, selling his stock in Apple to start his own company. However, he had recently come back on board as a consultant at $20,000 a year.

The Macintosh Plus and LaserWriter Plus had helped sales, along with a trade-in offer for old computers. PostScript, the computer language used by desktop publishing programs and printers, had ended up selling a lot of computers. Steve had been instrumental in bringing this about, pushing for its use and development, encouraging Adobe to use it for their printers and having Apple buy into the company to the tune of 20 percent. This proved to be remarkably prescient, just one occasion where he has driven the culture as much as tapped into it.

However, there wasn't the same excitement about Apple

that there had been. In fact, in some quarters, Apple was becoming something of a joke as they sought to regain their foothold in the personal computer business. 'Some analysts even laughed at Sculley's announcement that Apple might spend $15 million on a Cray supercomputer to help design future personal computers,' the Journal Record said. '"The Cray is going to be a waste of money," said DataQuest's Dave Fradin. "They hired some new computer scientists who want a new toy to play with. The idea of designing and simulating small computer programs on larger computers doesn't make sense. It's all for publicity."'

The Macintosh Plus did have one million bytes of memory, one of the three requirements of the 3M computer, but this only went so far in appeasing customers. 'However, analysts said the new computer still falls short of corporate needs by failing to provide an "open" design with internal expansion slots that would give it more versatility and power in performing business-related tasks. "Apple continues to tilt at windmills by trying to sell to the Fortune 500," said William Coggshall of Software Access, an industry market researcher. "It's not there and never will be there for them."'

Sculley confirmed that Apple would continue to target the education market, the company's foundation. Although they would sell to home users, Sculley said 'we're not interested in being a home computer company... I haven't seen anybody make any money since I've been in the industry being a home computer company.' Although the company was now making money on the back of the products Steve had helped design, it lacked what he had once brought to Apple: vision. Apple had become more conventional, more mundane without him. Although his departure had arguably been necessary for the immediate survival of the company, it left unanswered questions about their long-term strategy and product development.

Steve and Tina Redse finally broke up in 1989. Not long afterwards he met a woman called Laurene Powell at a Stanford lecture. Powell had been a trader for Goldman-Sachs, who was then attending Stanford Business School. He was so smitten with her that he cancelled the dinner he had planned with some of Apple's staff and took her out for a vegan meal instead. His sister Mona remembered talking to him about Laurene. 'I remember when he phoned the day he met Laurene. "There's this beautiful woman and she's really smart and she has this dog and I'm going to marry her."' The two remained an item ever since, although like his relationship with Redse theirs too was marked by extremes.

Steve wasn't capable of maintaining a consistently close romantic relationship with her, or anyone, in which he was vulnerable. So, for example, he proposed to Laurene on New Year's Day, 1990 – but didn't talk about it again for months after that. She moved in with him and became pregnant, but Steve could be so distant and emotionally unavailable that she moved out in disgust that September. Although they would eventually marry, the road there was by no means smooth. Maureen Dowd of the New York Times records of this time, 'He could be hard on women. Two exes scrawled mean messages on his walls. As soon as he learned that his beautiful, willowy, blonde girlfriend, Laurene Powell, was pregnant in 1991, he began musing that he might still be in love with the previous beautiful, willowy, blonde girlfriend, Tina Redse. He surprised a wide swath of friends and even acquaintances by asking them what he should do... "Who was prettier," he would ask, "Tina or Laurene?" And "who should he marry?"'

He and Laurene would finally tie the knot in March, 1991,

in a small Buddhist ceremony at Yosemite National Park.
They went on to have three children, starting with Reed that
September. He was an involved, hands-on dad, according
to Mona, although other sources have said that he could be
distant with his daughters, if not his son. 'Steve had been
successful at a young age, and he felt that had isolated him.
Most of the choices he made from the time I knew him were
designed to dissolve the walls around him. A middle-class boy
from Los Altos, he fell in love with a middle-class girl from
New Jersey. It was important to both of them to raise Lisa,
Reed, Erin and Eve as grounded, normal children. Their house
didn't intimidate with art or polish; in fact, for many of the
first years I knew Steve and Lo together, dinner was served
on the grass, and sometimes consisted of just one vegetable.
Lots of that one vegetable. But one. Broccoli. In season.
Simply prepared. With just the right, recently snipped, herb.'

Meanwhile, NeXT was hoping to change the field of
'intra-personal computing' with 1990's NeXTcube, the
NeXT Computer's successor. Steve's hope was that this
would revolutionise human communication with a new
system of sending email between computers. 'I think
we are three years ahead in pioneering this,' he said.

Although the idea of computers communicating via phonelines
had been around for some time, it had not yet caught on. In
May 1990 the New Straits Times wrote of the NeXTcube: 'The
key to interpersonal computing is multimedia electronic mail
(E-mail)'. Just 20 years ago, the term 'email' needed explaining
to the public. 'The NeXT cube comes with built-in networking
and E-mail facilities. Users can send electronic "letters"
complete with voice, image, graphics and full-motion video.
They can also add icons which, when activated, will launch
applications that automatically bring up associated files.'

Steve did not revolutionise computers themselves. Andy Hertzfeld argued that it was the microprocessor and Moore's law (the trend for the number of transistors capable of being placed on an integrated circuit to double every two years, thereby leading to similar increases in speed and power) is what democratized computing. 'It was inevitable from the advances in the semi-conductor industry and would have happened just as soon if there was no Steve.' Instead, Steve revolutionised what they did by using them in new ways. 'He said has not seen a more powerful tool for changing the way a company works,' continued the Straits' article.

Unfortunately, it wasn't enough. NeXT's computers weren't selling. Visionary though they might have been, they were expensive and badly positioned. They were far more powerful than any other personal computer on the market, but that was their weakness as much as their strength. The demand wasn't there. NeXT was burning through money, thanks to its expensive premises, staff and factory. In 1990 the company made just $28 million, with little hope of significant improvement. By 1993, NeXT had sold only 50,000 computers. A completely new strategy was needed.

5 | A change of direction

In the early 1990s, NeXT was a disaster, a money pit. Steve's dream of high-spec but affordable computers was not realisable at the time. Instead, the company changed direction and focused on software. Steve wound up the hardware division, laying off over half of NeXT's employees, so he could focus on the cutting-edge software solutions he was pioneering. One of these was the NeXTSTEP operating system, which was the first to use object-oriented programming – something that had enthused Steve when he first encountered it, and which he predicted would be widely used in the future. Then there was WebObjects, a platform that would later be used by many major companies to run online stores, including the Apple Store. Thanks to this reorganisation and change of emphasis, NeXT managed to turn a profit for the first time in its brief but expensive history.

Object-oriented programming was an innovation he had embraced because it allowed developers to write complex software in a fraction of the time of conventional programming, and with fewer problems. Steve believed that it would revolutionise software in the same way that Apple's computers had revolutionised hardware. Although it appears to be an arcane topic, of interest only to computer technicians and programmers, such was his reputation and enthusiasm that Rolling Stone magazine asked him to explain it in one interview. 'Objects are like people. They're living, breathing things that have knowledge inside them about how to do things and have memory inside them so they can remember things. And rather than interacting with them at a very low level, you interact with them at a very high level of abstraction, like we're doing right here,' he answered.

'Here's an example: If I'm your laundry object, you can give me your dirty clothes and send me a message that says, "Can you get my clothes laundered, please." I happen to know where the best laundry place in San Francisco is. And I speak English, and I have dollars in my pockets. So I go out and hail a taxicab and tell the driver to take me to this place in San Francisco. I go get your clothes laundered, I jump back in the cab, I get back here. I give you your clean clothes and say, "Here are your clean clothes."

'You have no idea how I did that. You have no knowledge of the laundry place. Maybe you speak French, and you can't even hail a taxi. You can't pay for one, you don't have dollars in your pocket. Yet I knew how to do all of that. And you didn't have to know any of it. All that complexity was hidden inside of me, and we were able to interact at a very high level of abstraction. That's what objects are. They encapsulate complexity, and the interfaces to that complexity are high level.'

This explanation is characteristic of Steve's brilliance, taking a complex subject of dubious relevance to the public and making it accessible and understandable. And he was right: object-oriented programming would prove to be the future. It contributed to turning NeXT around, and in doing so offered him the opportunity to return to Apple that he would not otherwise have had.

That was still some years away, though, and in the meantime NeXT wasn't the only thing that had been swallowing Steve's money. When he had left Apple, he sold almost all of his stock in the company in disgust. That meant he had cash resources of around $100 million. Aside from his 3M venture, he had bought George Lucas's computer graphics group in 1986, for the price of $10 million. The company would later be renamed Pixar.

Pixar was a hobby project for Steve, and without any major sources of revenue it sucked up his money for years. A little like NeXT, they were trying to develop both powerful computers for the movie industry, and the software to run on them. It was a small group of very talented people, and Steve was happy to keep them at arm's length and let them do their own thing.

Not long after he bought the division, they released the Pixar Image Computer. This was intended to appeal to specialist niches where computer visualisation was required: medicine, meteorology and geophysics, for example. Unlike the Macintosh or even the NeXT Computer, it was aimed at the very highest end of the commercial and scientific market, costing $135,000 (it also required a $35,000 workstation from Silicon Graphics or Sun Microsystems to run it). It was another visionary product, years ahead of its time, but although it sold to a number of labs and research facilities, it failed to ship in any significant volume. The next year, 1987, a redesigned machine sold for $30,000, although this also had limited appeal.

To make a little extra cash on the side, Pixar made a few animated commercials for TV. Its short films did gain some awareness within limited circles, but one animation, Tin Toy, won an Academy Award for Best Animated Short Film. The five-minute movie cost $300,000 and featured a toy's experiences of interacting with a young child. It was later included with the home video release of Toy Story. John Lasseter, Pixar's chief creative officer, began to gain quite a name for himself as an animator, but this and the small income derived from his creations weren't enough to justify Pixar's existence.

Realising that the company was going to continue to drain his resources unless something changed, Steve finally resolved to close down Pixar's hardware operations. Instead, he had them focus on RenderMan, a three-dimensional animation application that he believed would become the same standard for its industry that PostScript had become for desktop publishing. It wasn't that simple, though; mastering 3-D animation was phenomenally complicated. Pixar continued to rely on Steve for cash, coming out more than $8 million in the red in 1990.

Early in 1991, Steve threw down the gauntlet. He told them that he would only continue to bankroll Pixar if its employees returned all their shares in the company, effectively winding up the company as a public entity and making him the sole owner. He fired a large proportion of its staff, keeping only Lasseter's animation department and the programmers who made his work possible. This, after all, was the only part of Pixar to show any real promise of becoming profitable.

The early 90s were a period of uncertainty for Steve. Having lost Apple, it also appeared that he might lose NeXT and Pixar, too. There was a series of embarrassing compromises as he sought to dig NeXT out of its financial hole. This started with him licensing NeXTSTEP to run on IBM-compatible Intel processors. This development meant there was already a departure from NeXT's hardware, in which he had invested so much time, money and effort. Ultimately, this culminated in the complete closure of NeXT's hardware operations. The state of the art factory ended up with Canon, one of NeXT's investors, who promptly sold everything of value they could. Steve's dream had been to create a high-end machine that would put Apple's to shame and prove to be the future of computing. Instead, he was left with a small software company – one that made operating systems and other applications for Windows.

The news from Pixar wasn't any better. For a while things had been looking up. They had been hired by Disney to make an animated feature film, but work was slow and difficult, and Disney's execs weren't convinced by the project. They found characters unlikeable and the dialogue unsuitable for children. In 1993 they pulled the plug on the film, and Pixar was once again reduced to making TV commercials to get by.

These developments hit Steve hard. He was clearly depressed and stopped going to work. Instead, he stayed at home, playing with his young children. The preceding years had been first a period of trial, as he struggled to get his new company off the ground, followed by multiple perceived failures, betrayals and abandonments, as staff left and investors pushed things in directions he hated.

Perhaps surprisingly, what turned things around was the company that he had only bought as a curiosity to start with. Demoralised after Disney pulled the animation project, Steve had been trying to sell Pixar, without much success. Meanwhile, though, John Lasseter and his team had been pulling out all the stops. They rewrote the script for their film, Toy Story, and resubmitted it to Jeffrey Katzenberg, the Disney exec who had been instrumental in cancelling it in the first place. Katzenberg was impressed, and in February 1994 approved them to continue production. Initially, this wasn't enough for

Steve – at one point, he even considered selling the company to Microsoft. But he slowly started to come around to the idea that Pixar was going to become something that even he had not had the imagination to believe. His growing excitement about the project stirred him from his depression and convinced him that the company and its purpose still had a lot to offer.

The Register records the critical moment for Steve. 'The turnaround of Jobs' opinion of Pixar came when he attended a lavish Disney event in New York's Central Park in January of 1995 to showcase clips from two of that year's blockbuster animations: Pocahontas, scheduled for summer, and Toy Story, scheduled for the lucrative Thanksgiving time slot. Ralph Guggenheim, Toy Story's co-producer, told Alan Deutschman that "Steve went bonkers" at the attention that the Pixar film received at the event, which was attended not only by Disney's top execs, including CEO Michael Eisner, but also New York mayor and celeb Rudi Guliani, plus assorted other VIPs. "This was the moment when Steve realized the Disney deal would materialize into something much bigger than he had ever imagined," Guggenheim recalled, "and that Pixar was the way out of his morass with NeXT."'

Suddenly enthused, Steve jumped into the management of Pixar with both feet. He appointed himself President and CEO of the company, displacing the previous President Ed Catmull in the process. He also brought in a CFO from Wall Street firm EFI, to give the company an image overhaul ahead of the possibility of going public. A few weeks earlier, this would have been an insane prospect. An IPO would never attract the attention of investors; Pixar had swallowed millions upon millions of Steve's money for year after year, ever since he had first purchased it almost a decade earlier.

Everything changed when Toy Story premièred, with Steve suddenly credited as executive producer. Released on November 22, 1995, it surpassed all expectations. In its opening weekend alone – the three-day Thanksgiving slot – it made $28 million, recouping in that short time its entire $27 million investment. It would go on to top $160 at the US box office alone and more than $350 million worldwide. Pixar and Disney were both stunned. Steve, too, must have been incredulous, but the upside for him was even better. The IPO took place a week later, with shares priced at $22. During that day, they more than doubled to $49 at one point. It was the biggest IPO of the year. Steve's 80 percent stake in the company made him a billionaire. 'As David Price put it in The Pixar Touch, "Following the IPO, his shares of Pixar were valued at more than $1.1 billion – and the rounding error on that figure was almost as much as the entire value of his Apple holdings when he left Apple a decade earlier."'

Pixar's history since that point is well known. The company that had existed on Steve's credit for years and had nearly been sold or wound up many times went on to create hit after hit: A Bug's Life, Toy Story 2, Monsters, Inc. and Finding Nemo in its early years, and many more since. In 2006 Disney purchased the company for $7.4 billion of stock. Steve, who still owned 7 percent at this point, became Disney's biggest shareholder and joined the board of directors.

NeXT was still struggling, although the huge injection of Pixar cash for Steve had given him some breathing space. They were also positioned well for the future now, pioneering object-oriented programming far ahead of their main competition. But that wasn't necessarily enough to put them at the front, as Rolling Stone summarised of Steve's achievements in the field around that time: 'No one disputes the fact that

NeXT has a leg up on this new technology. Unlike most of its competitors, whose object-oriented software is still in the prototype stage, NeXTSTEP (NeXT's operating system software) has been out in the real world for several years. It's been road-tested, revised, refined, and it is, by all accounts, a solid piece of work. Converts include McCaw Cellular, Swiss Bank and Chrysler Financial. But as the overwhelming success of Microsoft has shown, the company with the best product doesn't always win. For NeXT to succeed, it will have to go up against two powerhouses: Taligent, the new partnership of Apple and IBM, and Bill Gates and his $4 billion-a-year Microsoft steamroller. "Right now, it's a horse race between those three companies," says Esther Dyson, a Silicon Valley marketing guru. A recent $10 million deal with Sun Microsystems – the workstation company that was once NeXT's arch rival – has breathed new life into NeXT, but it is only one step in a very long journey. Still, few dare count NeXT out.'

That three horse race would narrow to two when Apple approached NeXT with a view to buying the company. But as for Microsoft, the lumbering behemoth that had long been Steve's arch-rival (along with its founder, his 'frenemy' Bill Gates), Steve wasn't too worried about the competition they presented. 'Microsoft has had two goals in the last 10 years. One was to copy the Mac, and the other was to copy Lotus' success in the spreadsheet – basically, the applications business. And over the course of the last 10 years, Microsoft accomplished both of those goals. And now they are completely lost.'

A key part of their strategy had been to duplicate the Macintosh – something that had been relatively easy since Apple hadn't done much with it since Steve had left the company. 'They were able to copy the Mac because the Mac was frozen in time. The Mac didn't change much for the last 10 years. It changed maybe 10 percent. It was a sitting duck. It's amazing that it took Microsoft 10 years to copy something that was a sitting duck. Apple, unfortunately, doesn't deserve too much sympathy. They invested hundreds and hundreds of millions of dollars into R&D, but very little came out. They produced almost no new innovation since the original Mac itself. So now, the original genes of the Macintosh have populated the earth. Ninety percent in the form of Windows, but nevertheless, there are tens of millions of computers that work like that. And that's great. The question is, what's next? And what's going to keep driving this PC revolution?'

Even if Steve didn't rate Microsoft's chances of coming up with the next step in that revolution, their progress over the last ten years had threatened Apple. The problem was now becoming critical. Windows, the answer to the Mac's GUI, had proved a slow starter. It was appalling to start with, but changes over the years had gained ground, with 3.0 proving the turning point. Windows 95 was a game-changer, a massively popular release that severely undermined Apple's dominance and threatened to be a big nail in the company's coffin. Mac sales flat-lined, something that wasn't helped by the fact that Mac OS could be licensed by other computer makers. Inevitably, their profit margins weren't as high as Apple's, so consumers went elsewhere for their hardware knowing they could still get the Apple GUI experience.

Another problem was that high-quality new products simply weren't being designed any more. The personal computer industry wasn't attracting the same types of creative free-thinkers that it had been when Steve started out. Others have written about the way that 60s and 70s counterculture (including the drug culture) influenced the development of the

106

personal computer. Steve made the link himself, remarking that many of those who were most influential in the movement were poets, writers and musicians. Those people were leaving now and they weren't being replaced. 'They're not being attracted by something else. They're being driven out of the computer business. They're being driven out because the computer business is becoming a monopoly with Microsoft. Without getting into whether Microsoft gained its position legally or not – who cares? The end product of the position is that the ability to innovate in the industry is being sucked dry. I think the smartest people have already seen the writing on the wall. I think some of the smartest young people are questioning whether they'll really get in it. Hopefully things will change. It's kind of a dark period right now or that we're about to enter.'

One of Steve's talents was identifying the right blend of characteristics that made a product attractive and successful. He fully recognised that this synergy didn't happen very often – though he had been the driving force behind more than his fair share of examples. 'It seems to take a very unique combination of technology, talent, business and marketing and luck to make significant change in our industry. It hasn't happened that often,' he told Rolling Stone. Real changes tended to happen slowly, all things considered. 'The other interesting thing is that, in general, business tends to be the fueling agent for these changes. It's simply because they have a lot of money. They're willing to pay money for things that will save them money or give them new capabilities. And that's a hard one sometimes, because a lot of the people who are the most creative in this business aren't doing it because they want to help corporate America. The problem is, the psychology of the people who develop these things is just not going to enable them to put on suits and hop on planes and go to Federal Express and pitch their product.'

Real change – step-change, as it is known – requires the opportunities of big business. There weren't many people in the industry who could access that. Steve was one of them, a man who could communicate with investors and enthuse backers and major customers. 'To make step-function changes, revolutionary changes, it takes that combination of technical acumen and business and marketing – and a culture that can somehow match up the reason you developed your product and the reason people will want to buy it. I have a great respect for incremental improvement, and I've done that sort of thing in my life, but I've always been attracted to the more revolutionary changes. I don't know why. Because they're harder. They're much more stressful emotionally. And you usually go through a period where everybody tells you that you've completely failed.'

One example of the problem that he talked about was a PDA – personal digital assistant – that could send messages to other PDAs, a little like text-messaging. Whilst today we take this for granted – billions of text messages are sent every day – in the mid-80s it was a revolutionary idea. Apple's Newton was an early attempt to tap into the demand for such services, something Steve was pretty sure would fail simply on the grounds of price. Although they were designed for families to keep in contact, 'at $1,500 a pop with a cellular modem in them, I don't think too many people are going to buy three or four for their family. The people who are going to buy them in the first five years are mobile professionals.'

Apple was struggling. The restructuring and change of approach that had saved it ten years earlier had resulted in stagnation and a lack of vision. Between the time that Steve and Woz had started it in a garage and Steve had been sidelined and left – roughly ten years too – Apple had gone from nothing to being a billion-dollar company. It had grown further since then under Sculley's leadership, but Steve dismissed that growth compared to what had happened in his time there. 'Apple grew from nothing to two billion dollars while I was there. That's a pretty high growth rate. It grew five times since I left basically on the back of the Macintosh. I think what's happened since I left in terms of growth rate has been trivial compared with what it was like when I was there.' It wasn't the growth itself that had led to problems, but the attitude behind it. In one interview, Steve laid the blame for Apple's problems squarely at the feet of CEO John Sculley.

'What ruined Apple was values. John Sculley ruined Apple and he ruined it by bringing a set of values to the top of Apple which were corrupt and corrupted some of the top people who were there, drove out some of the ones who were not corruptible, and brought in more corrupt ones and paid themselves collectively tens of millions of dollars and cared more about their own glory and wealth than they did about what built Apple in the first place – which was making great computers for people to use.

'They didn't care about that any more. They didn't have a clue about how to do it and they didn't take any time to find out because that's not what they cared about. They cared about making a lot of money so they had this wonderful thing that a lot of brilliant people made called the Macintosh and they got very greedy and instead of following the original trajectory of the original vision – which was to make this thing an appliance, to get this out there to as many people as possible – they went for profits and they made outlandish profits for about four years.'

That was all fine for a while, but the party ended when Apple's competitors finally caught up with them and the company had nothing left to offer. 'What that cost them was the future. What they should have been doing was making reasonable profits and going for market share, which was what we always tried to do. Macintosh would have had a thirty-three percent market share right now, maybe even higher, maybe it would have even been Microsoft but we'll never know,' Steve told the Smithsonian Institution in April 1995. 'Now it's got a single-digit market share and falling. There's no way to ever get that moment in time back. The Macintosh will die in another few years and its really sad.' The Mac developers had left Apple, there was no one to create the next iconic product to take its place, and they were consequently living on borrowed time.

6 | Coming home

To give them their due, Apple and others in the industry knew this just as well as Steve did. The idea that Steve might return to Apple to take the helm and guide them away from the looming abyss first circulated in 1995. One industry boss – Oracle's Larry Ellison – mooted the thought of mounting a hostile takeover and installing Steve on the throne again. Steve himself torpedoed this; he didn't want it on those terms. He wanted them to ask him back. Perhaps he wanted them to grovel. Whatever, he knew they needed him now.

It wouldn't take place until the next year. The way it happened was beautiful, like the universe was working in harmony to make good some of Steve's old perceived mistakes. At the time, Apple was looking around for a new operating system. The Mac OS was old, and unsuited to the newer computers they were now producing. They needed something more powerful, but their own efforts to develop the right OS weren't progressing fast enough.

By this time, Sculley himself had been pushed out by Apple's board of directors after a series of bad products and the fallout from the lawsuit with Microsoft concerning their GUI. Michael Spindler took the helm in 1993, and was himself replaced in 1996 by Gil Amelio. Amelio developed the Taligent (a portmanteau of talent and intelligent) operating system, another object oriented OS, but the project stalled and so he started looking for other possibilities. There were one or two likely candidates, including one developed by Jean-Louis Gassée, the former Apple France exec who had shut down Steve's BigMac project after he left. He had started his own company, Be Inc., and his BeOS fit the bill for Apple. His price for the OS was $200 million.

This is another occasion on which Steve's legendary negotiating skills came into their own. Representatives of NeXT called Apple to tell them about NeXTSTEP, which was extremely highly regarded. Steve was initially unaware of their move and was amazed when he found out. However, he duly went to Apple for the first time in a decade and talked them into purchasing his company for the sum of $429 million. He received 1.5 million Apple shares and returned to the company he had founded as an informal adviser to Amelio. At the time, Apple's stock was trading at less than half what it had been 18 months earlier.

Apple had lost more than $1 billion in Amelio's time as CEO. Steve was not impressed with his new boss, and wasn't reticent in saying so to the press. He told Newsweek that Amelio had brought in a bunch of execs that he didn't need. 'I became aware... that the senior lieutenants Gil had surrounded himself with were not the people Apple should have,' he said. 'And the organization was pretty wacky.' Under the conditions of his return, Steve was not allowed to sell any of his new stock in Apple for six months. As soon as that period of time was up he sold all of his shares except for one. The move, dumping a large amount of Apple's stock on the market all at once, pushed prices even lower. Everyone assumed that it had been Steve, but he didn't admit it until an interview some time later. He told Time magazine, 'I pretty much had given up hope that the Apple board was going to do anything. I didn't think the stock was going up. If that upsets employees, I'm perfectly happy to go home to Pixar.'

'He sent a very, very strong statement to the board,' said Ken Lim, the editor of the CyberMedia 2001 newsletter. 'It may have been the impetus to give him the power to disband the board.' All of this made Amelio look pretty bad, but Steve claimed he had no interest in taking over – he had been offered the position and turned it down. 'People keep trying to suck me in. They want me to be some kind of Superman. But I have no desire to run Apple Computer. I deny it at every turn, but nobody believes me,' he said. Perhaps he believed that himself, perhaps it was his joke to himself. Or perhaps he really did think the CEO position was a poisoned chalice, that Apple was going to fail no matter what happened and he didn't want to be the one in charge when it did. Back in April 1996, Gil Amelio had said of his beleaguered company and his futile attempts to fix it, 'Apple is like a ship with holes in the bottom leaking water. My job is to get that ship pointed in the right direction.' (This was a quote later used by Steve himself.)

Steve didn't have an official role at Apple, but he did have influence. Several key decisions were made while he was still this kind of 'minister without portfolio'. Then, in July 1997, the inevitable happened. The board decided it was time for Amelio to go after just 17 months in the job. Amelio wasn't too sad about this – in all honesty, he must have felt like he was being let off the hook. Businessweek records, 'Early on a July workday in 1997, Jim McCluney, then head of Apple's worldwide operations got the call. McCluney was summoned with other top brass of the beleaguered company to Apple Computer

Inc's boardroom on its Cupertino campus. Embattled Chief
Executive Gil Amelio wasted no time. With an air of barely
concealed relief, he said: "Well, I'm sad to report that it's time
for me to move on. Take care," McCluney recalls. And he left.'

The board wanted Steve to become the new CEO
straight away, but he declined. The reasons he gave
were that he was already CEO of Pixar, and investors
and customers wouldn't have full confidence in him
if he was seen to be spreading himself too thin.

One move Steve made that was pretty controversial was a
partnership with Microsoft. Steve had previously been highly
critical of Bill Gates' company, and they had crossed swords
in the past. Steve saw Microsoft as unimaginative, monolithic
and so large that its monopoly posed a danger to the industry,
stifling competition. Then there was the personal problem with
them: back when Bill Gates had been working on software
to run on the Mac, Microsoft had managed to borrow the
Mac's GUI due to a contractual loophole, developing the
Windows platform that replicated the Mac's look and feel and
had eventually seriously undermined Apple's lead. In a 1996
documentary called Triumph of the Nerds, Steve had said,
'The only problem with Microsoft is they just have no taste.
I don't mean that in a small way. I mean that in a big way,
in the sense that they don't think of original ideas and they
don't bring much culture into their products.' Steve's problem
with Microsoft wasn't business or personal: it was both.

The animosity was mutual. Bill Gates didn't have a great
deal of respect for Steve, either – not because Apple's
computers or software weren't up to much, but because
Steve didn't have the technical background that he and
other key players in the industry did (had be been dealing

with Woz, it might have been another matter). When former CEO Gil Amelio told Gates that they were going to buy NeXT, thereby rehabilitating Steve into Apple, the Microsoft founder furiously replied, 'Don't you understand that Steve doesn't know anything about technology? He's just a super salesman… 99 percent of what he says and thinks is wrong. What the hell are you buying that garbage for?'

And so everyone was pretty surprised when, at the Macworld Expo in 1997, Steve announced a partnership with Microsoft. Gates' company would invest $150 million in Apple, as well as committing to releasing Microsoft Office for Macintosh for another five years. Many of the audience shared Steve's earlier views of Microsoft, and were appalled at the way he seemed to have sold out. It didn't help that Bill Gates appeared, his face projected on the huge screen behind Steve, to explain the deal. However, there were plenty of others present who realised that this endorsement and injection of cash had the potential to turn around the sinking ship that Apple had become.

It was still a bizarre move. Steve never would have contemplated it a few years earlier. Now, though, it seemed that it was time to put rivalry aside in the interests of pragmatism and saving the business that he had helped create. He explained this unexpected development: 'If we want to move forward and see Apple healthy and prospering again, we have to let go of a few things here. We have to let go of this notion that for Apple to win, Microsoft has to lose. We have to embrace a notion that for Apple to win, Apple has to do a really good job. And if others are going to help us that's great, because we need all the help we can get, and if we screw up and we don't do a good job, it's not somebody else's fault, it's our fault. So I think that is a very important perspective. If we want Microsoft Office on the Mac, we better treat the company that puts it out with a little bit of gratitude; we like their software. So, the era of setting this up as a competition between Apple and Microsoft is over as far as I'm concerned. This is about getting Apple healthy, this is about Apple being able to make incredibly great contributions to the industry and to get healthy and prosper again.'

The move received wider approval from shareholders when Apple's stock rose sharply as a result; Steve's decision to sell all his shares had turned out not be the most financially astute move of his career. He also later admitted that the presentation had been wrong, too. 'That was my worst and stupidest staging event ever. It was bad because it made me look small... and as if everything was in Bill's hands.'

Steve spent plenty of time justifying that particular initiative to the press, calling the naysayers in the Macworld audience who had booed him 'childish' and 'juvenile'. 'On the one hand, people are dying to get the latest release of Microsoft Office on their Macs, and on the other hand, they're booing the CEO of the company that puts it out. It seems really stupid to me,' he told Time. In an interview with Newsweek, he argued, 'It's crazy for the only two players on the desktop market not to be working together. It's a little like Nixon going to China. It's the right thing to do.'

There's no question that failure was high on his list of concerns. 'Apple has some tremendous assets,' he told Time, 'but I believe without some attention, the company could, could, could – I'm searching for the right word – could, could... Die.' Now adopting the label of 'interim CEO', he cut 70 percent of Apple's projects, pruning away the dross and keeping only those that he considered 'gems'. It didn't convince everyone, though. Michael Dell, the founder of Dell

Inc., was asked two months later what he would do if he was Apple's CEO. 'I'd shut it down and give the money back to the shareholders,' he replied. Apple still had a long way to go.

He went about the task of rescuing Apple with a will, making major changes in order to return the company to profitability. How much was his behaviour down to the formidable challenge, and how much was he asserting his authority on the company he had created but that had swept him out the door a decade earlier?

The story goes that a few minutes after Amelio received his marching orders, a dressed-down and relaxed-looking Steve strolled into the boardroom and dropped into a swivel chair. Rotating slowly in his seat, he asked the execs, 'O.K., tell me what's wrong with this place.' There were a few tentative answers, which he finally interrupted. 'It's the products! So what's wrong with the products?' Once again, there were a few stuttered attempts to answer the question, until he cut them off. 'The products suck!' Steve shouted at them. 'There's no sex in them any more!'

As interim CEO (or iCEO, as he would later joke) he started the long road to making Apple's products sexy again. Big changes were afoot. It wasn't just the company's products that Jobs would change: it was its very ethos, which he unceasingly moulded to his own personality. Employees had little choice: they could accept what was happening, as Steve recast the whole company, almost down to its DNA – or they could get out. He had been brought back again, for the price of $400 million. It hadn't been a hostile takeover. They had wanted him. They had kicked him out, improved but then floundered, come close to failing and finally begged him for help, installing him as their head. He had the mandate to do whatever he wanted.

The process started with Steve learning about every aspect and division of Apple once again. When he knew what everyone did, when he had discerned the intent and progress of every project, he would weigh them in the balance and pronounce them either work keeping or dead wood. These meetings were generally held in the boardroom which, as Salon.com described it, 'was in the only high-rise office building on the low-slung campus. It had a panoramic view of the expanse of Silicon Valley. Steve would call in the head of a product team and all of its key players. Anywhere from a dozen people to three dozen would crowd around the long wooden table. They had to show Steve all of their existing products and expound in detail about their future plans. If they made physical products, like monitors, they had to bring models of their upcoming lines. If they wrote software, they had to run Steve through the features of their programs.'

At this stage, it was a research exercise. Steve was gathering data about his company, putting all the pieces together in his mind until he knew the big picture and could form a strategy. There was little confrontation, but everyone felt there was something in the air, something urgent and threatening, like a line of schoolchildren waiting outside the headmaster's office. His power was absolute; Amelio had made some tough cuts to staff and projects, but everyone knew there was more coming and they would all have to justify their existence.

There was usually a series of meetings with each group. In the first, he would simply listen, gathering information. In the second, he would challenge them: 'If you had to cut half your products, what would you do?' Sometimes, he would ask them what they would do if their funds were unlimited. In this way, speaking to group after group, Steve met directly with almost everyone at the company. In the early days it had been a tight-knit outfit and it had been possible to know all the employees and deal with them in person. Now that Apple had many hundreds of employees, that should have been impossible, but no one seemed to have told Steve this. Sculley had reorganised the company, giving it a far more orthodox corporate structure. Steve rode roughshod over this, ignoring the standard protocols and going direct to the people he wanted to talk to without asking their managers. 'Steve has the ability to buffer so much in his head,' one employee explained. 'He can remember the last conversation and the last e-mail exchange that he had with 300 people.'

During this period he showed his brilliance as well as his erratic and sometimes grating temperament. He was incredibly demanding, especially of his execs. One, Heidi Roizen – now a Silicon Valley venture capitalist – was relentlessly bombarded with messages on her home and cellphone, as well as her pager and at her office. It would start around seven in the morning, almost every day of the week. When she became concerned that Steve's constant questions and haranguing would prove too much for her, she decided to ignore the calls and communicate only by email. She spoke to another member of the board, Bill Campbell, who was suffering the same treatment. 'Do what I do,' she advised him. 'Don't answer the phone.'

'That's what my wife said. I tried that,' he replied. 'But then Steve would come over to my house. He lives only three blocks away.' When Heidi suggested he simply didn't answer the door, he responded, 'I tried that. But my dog sees him and goes berserk.' Steve's standards were astronomically high, he expected the utmost from his execs, and he absolutely refused to take no for an answer. One way or another, he was going to hammer Apple and its people into shape. The only danger was that he would break them along the way.

Steve was looking for 'sexy' products, and he found what he was after pretty quickly. It is illustrative of his approach that it wasn't the hardware or software that inspired him to begin with: it was the aesthetics of the box. In his last incarnation as Apple's CEO, Steve had made some choices that had frustrated and infuriated his more technically-minded employees. He had forced the Apple III team to make their hardware fit in the shape and style of case he had decided, without any thought to the practicalities of it. That had been one of the reasons the Apple III failed so badly; the restrictions of the design caused overheating problems. Then there was the Macintosh; Steve had forced the team to compromise on sound quality because he didn't want anyone drilling a hole in his beautiful case, even if it did circumvent the distortion problems that otherwise occurred.

In this instance, the object of his affections was a large lump of polystyrene designed by a man called Jonathan Ive. It was a model for what would become the 'iMac', or internet Macintosh. At this stage, that was all he had: the design. The electronics, what the machine could actually do – that was all up for grabs. But he did have an idea of the competition. 'Steve's thinking was strongly influenced by his friendship with Larry Ellison as well as their unspoken rivalry. He believed the future belonged to stripped-down machines, called "network computers," or NCs, that would connect to the Internet and cost only half as much as PCs. Larry had even started his own company, Network Computer Inc., to try to cash in on the idea. Steve decided that the iMac would be a network computer. "We're going to beat Ellison at his own game," he told his Apple colleagues, who were surprised to see Steve secretly delighting in the competition with his best friend.'

For every product that enthused him, there were dozens that didn't make the grade. One of the big initiatives he took was to end the situation where Macintosh software could be licensed by third parties, thereby ending both the problem and opportunity of cheap clones. As he cancelled the ones he deemed a drain on Apple's resources, many employees learned to avoid him, fearful that they would become the latest casualties of the purge. The stories go that the staff developed a collective reluctance to take the elevator with him, 'afraid that they might not have a job when the doors opened,' as one account goes. (There was one elevator in Steve's building that had protective covers on its walls because some construction was being carried out. One employee remarked, 'This must be Steve's elevator, since it's padded.' Another replied, 'Is it for him or for us?') In fact, there were comparatively few such 'summary executions' – but they passed into legend and became part of the atmosphere of the company.

But design wasn't Apple's major problem: it was image. They somehow needed to regain the cool they'd had a decade earlier. Steve had stripped the company down to a handful of 'gems' as he termed them; Amelio had reduced their R&D from 350 to 50 projects, and Steve winnowed that down to just 10. Now, they needed to make the most of what they had. Since the mid-1980s, they had lost their hip image. And who better to help them regain it than Chiat-Day, who had come up with the iconic 1984 advert that, against all of the board's expectations, had proved such a colossal hit?

As it happened, Chiat-Day still had the same creative director that Steve had worked with 13 years earlier. Lee Clow argued that Apple had moved on from its early days, but that they could still project the same kind of spirit. The analogy he drew was with Harley Davidson, which managed to bestow a kind of renegade spirit on its customers, even if they were wealthy bankers now. Steve had been inspired by Nike, who managed to communicate a sense of dynamism and athleticism that had nothing to do with displaying their shoes. It was all in the marketing. Apple needed just that kind of conduit to its fan base.

So it was that Clow came up with Apple's new slogan: 'Think Different'. They designed a one-minute commercial that featured still black-and-white images of 17 different iconic personalities of the 20th century. Many of these were figures that Steve had displayed on posters in his home – one of the reasons the idea appealed to him in the first place. It resonated with him, as he believed it would with others. The world-changers in the advert were Albert Einstein, Bob Dylan, Martin Luther King Jr., Richard Branson, John Lennon with Yoko Ono, Buckminster Fuller, Thomas Edison, Muhammad Ali, Ted Turner, Maria Callas, Mahatma Gandhi, Amelia Earhart, Alfred Hitchcock, Martha Graham, Jim Henson with Kermit, Frank Lloyd Wright and Pablo Picasso.

The idea of the advert was to encourage customers to return to Apple, the original rebel – the little personal computer company that had taken on the likes of IBM, against all odds, and changed the world. Steve wanted to foster that spirit among Apple's fan base again, making the company feel like the natural choice for unconventional culture-shifters. The text ran, 'Here's to the crazy ones. The misfits. The rebels. The troublemakers. The round pegs in the square holes. The ones who see things differently. They're not fond of rules. And they have no respect for the status quo. You can quote them, disagree with them, glorify or vilify them. About the only thing you can't do is ignore them. Because they change things. They push the human race forward. While some may see them as the crazy ones, we see genius. Because the people who are crazy enough to think they can change the world, are the ones who do.'

On the last day of September, 1997, he threw a party – with vegetarian food – for all his employees, to celebrate the launch of the new campaign. Assembling the staff, he said, 'Apple spends $100 million a year on advertising, and it hadn't done us much good.' They were still going to spend the same amount of money, he said, they were just going to make it count now. Apple had to work smarter, not harder. It wasn't just about the technical spec of their computers – or even primarily about their computers at all. It was all about their image.

The fact was that Apple's marketing department was in a mess, and had been for years. Until they brought Steve back in, the marketing staff had been so poor that the engineers would actually leak developments of their own projects to the press, believing that this was the only way they would get any real publicity. One of Steve's first moves was to stamp that out, implementing a 'loose lips sink ships' policy. This enraged the staff, who had grown accustomed to doing things their own way and hated having this kind of edict dictated to them. A handful of on-the-spot dismissals when he had been unimpressed with a project (proclaiming 'This is shit!' and firing the people responsible) led to a culture of fear and suspicion.

But bizarrely, it all started to work. The problem was that things at Apple had got stale. The company was running on autopilot, going through the motions and getting by but not doing anything spectacular. Steve once again stamped his personality on the company, and anyone who didn't like it knew where the door was. The complacency that had reigned for years now was over, one way or another. 'It was filled with people who had virtually ignored and ultimately outlasted three CEOs as they did their own things,' records Salon. '"I don't know if the previous CEOs at Apple had any effect on that company," says John Warnock of Adobe, which is Apple's biggest software provider. "We would have meetings with all those CEOs and nothing would happen, no traction, unless the group responsible went for the idea. The energy just dissipated into the organization, where the first person capable to make a decision is the one who makes it. But with Steve, he comes in with a very strong will and you sign up or get out of the way. You have to run Apple that way – very direct, very forceful. You can't do it casually. When Steve attacks a problem, he attacks it with a vengeance. I think he mellowed during the NeXT years and he's not so mellow any more."'

'Think Different' might have been Apple's new motto, but Steve was fiercely imposing discipline and his own set of standards on the company. They could think different: it just had to be his different. That extended far beyond the projects and marketing. The relaxed atmosphere at Apple ended. Once upon a time, employees had wandered around outside, smoking and talking, and even playing with their dogs, which they brought into work. 'Steve enforced new rules. He decreed that there would be no smoking anywhere on the Apple property. Then he banned dogs on campus, ostensibly because canines were messy and some people were allergic to them. The employees were outraged: Why didn't Steve understand them? Smoking in the courtyard was how they networked with their colleagues from other departments. It was a vital form of communications! Steve's prohibitionism forced them to take long walks to De Anza Boulevard so they would be off the Apple property. It wasted a lot of time.' To be fair, there were some good reasons why employees had been bringing their pets in and keeping a relaxed work environment. Many of them worked very long hours, giving more to Apple than they would in any regular job. A bit of latitude seemed only fair when they hardly spent any quality time at home.

But Steve kept looking at the bigger picture. At one meeting, he was asked what he thought the worst feature of Apple was. Steve thought about it and answered, 'The cafeteria.' Then he fired its staff and brought in a chef from Il Fornaio, a classy Italian restaurant in Palo Alto, who soon had not the employees' but Steve's favourite dishes on the menu. Salon concluded, 'Somehow, the reign of terror was beginning to work. Apple had long been like a civil-service bureaucracy, with thousands of entrenched employees who did pretty much whatever they wanted regardless of which political appointees were temporarily at the top. Now that was changing. People started to realize that Steve could assert his authority over seemingly any aspect of the company's life. Apple was going to follow the vision of a single person, from the no-smoking rules and the healthy cuisine to the editing of the TV advertisements. Steve was clearly in charge, and Steve was seemingly everywhere.' Perhaps it struck some of the older employees as ironic that the '1984' ad had featured Apple as the freedom fighter who brought down the futuristic dictatorship, because now Steve was that Big Brother, dictating company policy and micro-managing down to the level of the food people could eat.

The management style worked for Steve. Like his Who's Who of cultural icons, he was an innovator: he set, rather than followed the trend – as illustrated by the Wayne Gretzky quote he loved: 'I skate to where the puck is going to be, not where it has been.' Returning to the position of CEO gave him freedom to do pretty much what he wanted. It didn't necessarily make him popular: he was a demanding perfectionist. But somehow, it worked.

One author, Jeffrey Young, spoke to ABC about how Steve could be simultaneously infuriating and inspiring. 'Steve is a perfectionist, but he's also a perfectionist with taste and so because he's a perfectionist with taste he can drive people who have great talent to do things beyond what they might be able to do otherwise. And that's what he does: he inspires you to show him up. One of Steve's favourite phrases is "brain dead" and he would say that about you no matter almost what you were doing. If he thought something was stupid he'd tell you it was brain dead. And he said this over and over and it became his sort of pet phrase.

'And you know he would tell everybody this that he hated: you were brain dead. "That was a brain dead idea." "It was a brain dead decision." "It was a brain dead design." And that intensity that pursued you all the time either drove you to do greater and greater stuff, to go way beyond anything you could ever do before. Or it drove you to leave because you couldn't stand it.'

Whilst Steve had some knowledge of electronics, he was never the designed Woz had been. But what he did know was what everything cost – and how to negotiate a lower price. 'He knew what parts to buy. He knew the price of every part in the Apple I and Apple II and he was famous in Silicon Valley for telling people to sharpen their pencils, to get a better deal, to shave a penny, a tenth of a cent, off a component. People don't remember that part of Steve. But Steve was an extraordinarily good manufacturing guy and operations guy. He could make computers really cheaply. That's a very important skill, something that Apple has always done well with. They've always had very high margins and their products are highly priced but their margins have always been good because their cost of goods is always remarkably low.'

Steve put this skill to good use by reinvigorating the companys' Power Mac and PowerBook computers with new chips designed by Motorola, hoping to outclass the Pentium-based products of the company's chief competitors. Then, in 1998, he unveiled the first project he had overseen in his new role: the iMac.

Introducing his new baby in May of that year, he proclaimed it 'gorgeous'. Whilst some saw this as little more than hype, the market disagreed: the iMac would be the fastest-selling Macintosh ever, returning Apple to profit and cementing it and Steve as forces to be reckoned with.

In its original form the iMac was little more than an egg-shaped monitor, the evolution of the chunk of foam he had been seen carrying around a few months earlier, designed by a Londoner called Jonathan Ive. The concept was an all-in-one desktop computer, with no separate tower; all the processing would be carried out by the components hidden behind the CRT display. As the technology progressed, this would further develop into a sleek flat screen with the components in its base, before further advances made it possible to put them within the slim housing of the flat screen itself. At the time, it was yet another revolutionary idea. As one exec commented, 'A lot of people are going to be asking, "Where did the rest of the computer go?"'

Aesthetics was as important as ever; Steve's claim was that the back of the iMac was more attractive than the front of his competitors' computers. Even the power button was kept out of sight to avoid spoiling its lines. A 'sleep' light pulsed gently at the front, like the rhythm of calm breathing. The monitor housing itself was a translucent, curved blue-green design, an organic shape against the ubiquitous beige boxes of the time. Like the Mac before it, and the Mac OS operating system, this innovation proved a strong influence on the computer industry, and many others. Curves and soft colours became cool – a phenomenon seen in products as far-ranging as cookware and coops for urban chicken keepers.

7 | 'i' is for lifestyle

Apple was back on the map, with Steve the man of the hour. The iMac sold two million units in just two years. Its popularity prompted a new wave of software developers to return to creating programmes for Apple, further increasing momentum. This was a critical factor in competing with Windows, which had far more software available.

One of the most far-reaching innovations of the iMac was not its design, but its branding. The 'i' stood for 'internet', but came to mean so much more. It was truly a personal computer, the 'i' tapping into the growing spirit of individualism and personal experience, first seen in the 90s but coming of age a decade later. What it suggested was that the 'i' was the centre of the world. It was brilliantly illustrative of the Zeitgeist, as technology and culture drove each other to create a range of products designed as lifestyle pieces for the individual. Arguably, this culminated in the iPod and iPhone phenomenon, as convergence allowed everything from personal communication, web browsing, social networking, photography, music and more to be accessed from the same hand-held device, which was essentially treated as an extension of the self.

If there is one legacy that Steve has that has changed out culture more than any other but that has been underestimated, perhaps this is it. Just that one small letter, the 'i' that became a mainstay of Apple's branding, has come to epitomise Generation Y. User experience was always key for Apple, and Steve sometimes flogged this horse so hard that it died (as with the aesthetic attractions of the Apple III that actually prevented it from working properly). The emphasis on the self was something that this 'i' both captured and fostered, amplifying a generational trend and turning it into something approaching a religion for the millennium. One writer, Dale Kuehne, even used the term 'iWorld' as a shorthand for the post-modern culture of individualistic consumerism that now pervades the West. Some have identified this as a harmful trend, others believe its values of choice and change are the highest good. Whatever side of the fence you come down on, one thing is clear: you can't deny the impact it has had on the world. Like Steve's icons in the Think Different advert, it's impossible to ignore the incredible impact that 'i', and everything it stands for, has had on the world.

As a product geared towards personal experience, ease of use was key – something that was emphasised in a popular commercial starring Jeff Goldblum. The idea was that only two steps were necessary to use the computer: take it out of the box and connect it to the internet. 'There's no step 3!' Goldblum declared. The commercial was called 'Simplicity Shootout' and compared the progress made by two people setting up their respective computers: a seven-year-old boy (and his dog) with an iMac, against a Stanford MBA student with an HP Pavilion 8250. Of course, the boy finished first, while the MBA was still struggling at the end of the ad.

Functionality was the iMac's big selling point, just as Apple had excited first homebrew enthusiasts and then the general public in its early days. Something curiously analogous was happening in the late 1990s, 20 years after Steve and Woz had founded Apple. Computers were cool but still, at this point, the preserve of the initiated. It was the early days of the internet, just as the web was gaining critical mass. Email and web-access were becoming mainstream, appearing as standard in universities and workplaces, but access was still clunky, without the intuitive control we now take for granted. Telnet and other systems required arcane combinations of keypresses, patience and engagement to work. There was a gap in the market – a gaping hole – to make the most powerful technology in a generation available to everyone. Steve was a trailblazer, and had been here once before. He was well-placed to pull off the same trick twice.

The iMac was the biggest computer story of 1998. It sat perfectly in Steve's ethos of rule-breaking and culture-setting. Many reviews were excellent; others hated it. But one way or another, the new computer was being talked about. WAP magazine listed some of the iMac's most notable features (proclaiming it 'cute' and an 'attractive nuisance' along the way, thanks to its tendency to stall office productivity when everyone wanted a go and they only had one to play with):
For Internet gossipmongers, it was a major defeat: there were no leaks prior to Steve Jobs' announcement of the iMac in May 1998. This pretty much confirms suspicions about their reporting skills;
For Apple bashers, it was proof: nobody would buy this funny looking blue thing. Some probably still believe that;
For proponents of network computing, it was a milestone: the iMac was arguably the first mass-market computer ever designed to be network-centric, with a fast built-in modem, a very fast built-in Ethernet port, and no obsolete, virus-

passing floppy disk drive. This is turning out to be true;
For Mac traditionalists, it was a mistake: the iMac didn't
have a SCSI port, a LocalTalk port, a serial port or a floppy
disk drive. Some probably still believe that, too;
For computer novices, it was an opportunity: 'I
want that blue computer that can get you on the
Internet in 15 minutes.' Hundreds of thousands
of novice opportunists came away happy.

One of the most controversial features was the lack of a floppy
disk drive. Floppy disks were one of Steve's personal bugbears.
He hated them. That was more or less the only reason he didn't
want one on the iMac. At the time, every other computer had a
floppy disk drive. They would eventually be made obsolete, but
in 1998 we certainly weren't there yet. It wasn't the only such
decision he made. Some years later he decided to pull CD and
DVD drives from MacBooks, and deciding not to support Adobe
Flash on the iPhone and iPad. These moves were often viewed
as odd or frustrating, at best, but the industry followed sooner
or later. Now, legacy-free PCs, without the floppy disk drive,
have been the standard for 10 years. It was a dying technology;
Apple just saved some money by removing something no one
had yet realised they didn't need. The exception might just be
Adobe Flash, which is still extremely common. Steve claimed
the reason he didn't want it on the iPad was that it was a
'buggy' battery-drainer made by lazy programmers. In fact, it
was a little more personal than that. In 1999, when he was
looking for software for the iMac, he approached Adobe for
help with a video editing suite. They declined – despite the fact
that the relationship went years back, with Steve investing in
the company and encouraging them to create the PageMaker
programme that would help bring about the desktop publishing
revolution. He was livid. 'I put Adobe on the map and they
screwed me,' he said. Dropping Flash was a quid pro quo.

Steve would follow the iMac's fantastic success by focusing on a very deliberate product range over the next two years: regular and high-end desktop and laptop/notebook computers using the same technology, meaning that Apple now had at least one thing for everyone: iMac, Power Mac, iBook and PowerBook. Apple also moved into Wi-Fi, then an emerging technology, pioneering another phenomenon that would quickly become an industry standard.

Steve eventually accepted full CEO status, having proved that he could manage Pixar and Apple at the same time, and now knowing that the company's fortunes were on the up. He no longer risked being the man at the helm when Apple sank for good.

One of the most significant developments he ushered in around this time was the Mac OS X. It was called 'X' because it was the tenth major OS version, but also something very new. The X was also a nod to its Unix origins – hence it was pronounced OS 'X' not 'ten' (though Steve initially called it 'ten' at Macworld 2000). This was a new operating system, an evolution of the Mac OS but also based on NeXTSTEP, redesigned for the Mac – thereby alienating neither group. One of its most significant functions was true multi-tasking. In simple terms, this meant that it could switch processing power between applications whilst protecting the memory that they used, to avoid them crashing the computer. Functionally, this was a leap forwards from the old OS. Aesthetically, too, it showed Steve's hand behind the scenes. The most obvious change in appearance was the 'Aqua' theme. This included 'soft edges, translucent colors, and pinstripes – similar to the hardware design of the first iMacs'. The effect was startling when presented to users who were used to the conventional

Mac OS look. Steve himself was particularly pleased with it and noted his priority that it should better than any other OS as well as work better. 'One of the design goals was when you saw it you wanted to lick it,' he said at the Macworld conference.

Of course, like any such innovation it attracted its fair share of criticism as well as acclaim. Writing for the Ars Technica blog, John Syracusa said, 'That's not to say that it was perfect – far from it. Some judged it too bright; the pinstripes were a bit too pronounced; translucency hindered legibility in some areas; the list went on. These flaws were slowly corrected with each subsequent revision of Mac OS X. But while these corrections improved the usability and (usually) the look of the OS, they also compromised the overall aesthetic design. What started as a (flawed) work of genius was patched and filled and tweaked by a committee of pragmatists, rendering it much improved, but considerably less inspired.'

OS X went out early in 2001 and consolidated Apple's recovery from the slump it had suffered in the 90s. This was a supreme irony and another beautiful twist: that the company Steve had been pushed out of well over a decade earlier had been saved from extinction by an operating system designed by a company he only formed in response to his departure.

The millennium was another watershed for personal computing. Not due to the Y2K problem, which turned out to be more or less a non-event. It was rather that personal computing gained critical mass at this point. The internet was coming of age, offering possibilities that few had imagined possible only a decade before.

Towards the end of the millennium, many experts started to see a movement that they considered would become the norm: a trend away from the personal computer as it was known at the time towards an internet-based phenomenon. In the near future, the theory went, personal computers would be no more than stripped down terminals, the only purpose of which was to connect users to the vast quantities of information, software and content available over the internet. The expectation was that the development of PCs would stagnate, since they were no longer necessary.

Steve thought otherwise. As he saw it, the personal computer had undergone a process of evolution over the preceding 20 years that was far from complete. To begin with, in the 1980s, computers had been used predominantly in a business and organisational context – the success of the Apple II and VisiCalc had largely been down to this kind of use. The 1990s saw something different, with software appealing to creative users and then internet and email revolutionising personal communication. Now, they had entered a third age, where PCs were the 'Digital Hub', as he called it, of entire lives. Technology had progressed to the point where all kinds of equipment was available to the public, from cameras to music devices. These all relied on a computer to download, organise and disseminate material. That meant it was the indispensable centre of the digital age. This phenomenon was arguably most visibly vindicated when Apple brought out the iPod: the very symbol of the revolution in personal digital devices.

The point of the 'digital hub' strategy was to make the personal computer the focal point of consumers' lives, rather than the cloud model that other future-gazers had predicted. iTunes was a major strand of this: a media centre that would download, organise and play music and other media files. iTunes was a master stroke, though Steve argued that Apple was simply doing what he had always intended it to do: making computers beautiful, functional and easy to use. 'The great thing is that Apple's DNA hasn't changed,' he said. 'The place where Apple has been standing for the last two decades is exactly where computer technology and the consumer electronics markets are converging. So it's not like we're having to cross the river to go somewhere else; the other side of the river is coming to us.'

In fact, he nearly missed the boat. The digital music revolution was under way and Steve suddenly realised he was late to the party. Sites like Napster were all the rage, and young people were busy ripping their CD collections onto their computers and illegally sharing them with each other. Apple had nothing to tap into this phenomenon.

That would have been a missed opportunity – and one that would have unthinkably changed the way we deal with downloadable music – had Steve and the Apple team not pulled all the stops out. The platform for iTunes already existed thanks to his work at NeXT, but the full software was completed in just five months.

The allure of iTunes would all come together when the iPod was introduced. This was Steve's genius: not that he created something new – the iPod wasn't. MP3 players already existed, and more cheaply. As in so many other cases, the innovation was to make an existing technology user-friendly, accessible and therefore better than any of the competition's – realising and then applying potential that no one else saw.

The first iPod was better than its competition for a number of reasons. It was beautifully designed, for a start; Jonathan Ive, who had designed the iMac and many of Apple's subsequent products, had outdone himself. But then there was its functionality. The fact was that existing MP3 players weren't any good. As one Apple exec noted, 'The products stank.' The problem was that they rarely had much capacity – usually no more than a few CDs. Additionally, they were either large and unwieldy, or small and fiddly. Battery life was typically terrible, and transfer speeds for moving music from computer to device were appalling.

Wired.com relates how Steve learned of the potential and moved – fast. '"I don't know whose idea it was to do a music player, but Steve jumped on it pretty quick and he asked me to look into it," said Jon Rubinstein, the veteran Apple engineer who's been responsible for most of the company's hardware in the last 10 years.' Fast-moving cellphone technology meant that better batteries and displays were being developed constantly. Plus, Apple had many of the pieces already in place. 'We didn't start from scratch,' Rubinstein said. 'We've got a hardware engineering group at our disposal. We need a power supply, we've got a power supply group. We need a display, we've got a display group. We used the architecture team. This was a highly leveraged product from the technologies we already had in place.'

The nature of the parts meant that the rough shape was obvious from the start – a neat oblong box that beat the competition for size and weight from the start. All the same, Steve made Ive and his team work hard, creating a line of prototypes to see what would look best. 'Steve made some very interesting observations very early on about how this was about navigating content,' Ive said. 'It was about being very focused and not trying to do too much with the device – which would have been its complication and, therefore, its demise. The enabling features aren't obvious and evident, because the key was getting rid of stuff.' One of the best features was the click wheel which, along with the iPod's interface, made browsing through dozens of songs extremely simple. That would be important, since the five gigabyte drive offered huge storage: 'a thousand songs in your pocket', as Apple promoted their new device. One of the best innovations was perfect integration with iTunes – all you had to do was plug it into your computer.

The iPod was an unbelievable success. Originally an Apple-only product, it was later made Windows compatible to access those users, allowing them to see what Apple technology could do rather than forcing them to make the change. Steve's negotiating talent came to the fore again as he sealed a deal with the music companies, agreeing on a price of just $0.99 per track and $9.99 for whole albums. That way, Apple wouldn't receive much from the labels, but the low prices would attract customers and power iPod sales through the stratosphere.

The result exceeded anyone's expectations. When the iTunes music store was opened, it sold five million songs in less than two months, and another eight million in the next three. iTunes accounted for 70 percent of legal music downloads, despite the fact that at this point, it was only available on the Mac.

Steve's strategy of seducing Windows users back to Apple was complemented by another bold marketing plan – one that many analysts saw as tantamount to insanity but that miraculously worked, and has done ever since. Like personal computers, the high street had long been assumed to be in slow and inexorable demise. The internet had made physical shops obsolete: iTunes had already proved that, making purchasing music as easy as clicking a button. It wouldn't take long before stores like HMV started feeling the pinch as customers browsed online rather than among the physical racks of CDs. Bricks and mortar stores had seen their day, especially in the digital realm.

So why was Apple branching out and opening big, high-profile stores in prime locations on the high street? These stores were prominent and expensive – surely black holes for cash. Analysts predicted they would fail. Incredibly, though, they proved to be a shrewd move. In keeping with the 'i' theme, these weren't just shops. They were Lifestyle centres: places where customers could go and browse, try out Apple's products, get to know the company and how it could serve their needs and desires. They were yet another outworking of Steve's incisive and visionary grasp of the culture. They were accompanied by the 'Get a Mac' TV campaign, which aggressively targeted PC users and tried to attract them over to Apple. The adverts were very simple, featuring two people well-known in each of the airing locations – typically actors and comedians. They would introduce themselves, 'I'm a Mac' and 'I'm a PC', and then give a brief summary of their characteristics. PCs were presented as conventional, formal and a bit tedious, whereas Macs were innovative and exciting. The series of adverts included many that openly mocked Microsoft and its products.

The iPod sealed Steve's position as an icon of individualism and millennial culture. It represented hardware, software and aesthetics coming together seamlessly to answer a need that was barely apparent before it existed. Other companies couldn't combine these things, and they didn't have the vision for how to use that synergy anyway. It was followed with the Mini and Shuffle, moving into the territory occupied by other MP3 players but doing it better. These would later be supplemented by the iPod Nano and Video. As iTunes was rolled out across the world, it dominated the online music market and attracting offline shoppers away from physical shops onto their online store.

8 | The end of an era

Thanks to this series of shrewd moves, Apple was going from strength to strength. But Steve was not well. In October 2003 he had a routine scan and the doctors discovered a tumour on his pancreas. Pancreatic cancer is one of the worst cancers, usually fast to progress and with a very poor prognosis for survival. Steve was lucky, though: it turned out he had a rare kind, one which is diagnosed just a few hundred times a year in the US: neuroendocrine tumor or islet cell carcinoma. The prognosis with this is much better and it can often be successfully treated with surgery to remove the growth.

Surgery was necessary, but Steve initially refused. The reason seems to have been something that went to the heart of his personality and was responsible for many of his most notable traits, good and bad. His apparently unshakeable self-belief lent him so many characteristics – perfectionism, stubbornness, abrasiveness and inability to tolerate 'bozos'. It may also have ultimately killed him.

He eschewed conventional medicine for the Eastern mysticism he had explored during his time at Atari. One of his close friends and business partners, Avie Tevanian, referred to the 'reality distortion field' that Bud Tribble had talked about back in his Mac years in the early 1980s, 20 years earlier. 'Steve was an unconventional person and when it came to treating his illness he was very happy to use non-traditional methods. I think he truly thought that through some unconventional means he could cure himself.'

Instead of trusting the doctors, Steve opted for a special diet. 'Being Steve, it was easy for him to find people who would agree that it was worth a try. Many of us around him, myself included, his wife and other people were saying: "Steve, you know, maybe you should just have some surgery here and get it over with,"' Tevanian told the BBC. 'He was the kind of person that could convince himself of things that weren't necessarily true or necessarily easy, maybe easy is the better way to think of it. That always worked with him for designing products, where he could go to people and ask them to do something that they thought was impossible. But he would keep asking and say: "You know, it's impossible but I still want you to try" – and because of his sheer will, they would actually make it happen, or make something like it happen.' That strategy couldn't and wouldn't work when it came to his health.

He ignored the advice of his friends, family and colleagues for nine months, until he was finally forced to admit that his strategy – which, according to some sources, included 'wacky fruit diets, hydrotherapy, a psychic and expressing his negative feelings', acupuncture, huge quantities of fruit juice and 'treatments he found on the internet' – wasn't working. He later said that the reason he had persisted was simple denial. 'I really didn't want them to open up my body, so I tried to see if a few other things would work out,' he said. His wife later explained, 'He has that ability to ignore stuff he doesn't want to confront. It's just the way he's wired.'

Surgery is the first form of treatment tried for islet cell carcinoma. Even if this doesn't work, there are other possibilities. One surgeon, David Levi, commented to WebMD on the condition: 'If it can be cured with surgery we try for that. If not there are options: chemotherapy and a number of other options to try to control this tumor. Some of these cancers are not curable, but patients can do well for years and years... Many can be treated medically for months and years and do quite well and lead normal lives to the last.' Steve's surgery was extensive; the 'Whipple procedure', as it is known, involves removing the head of the pancreas along with part of the bile duct, gall bladder and small intestine, and sometimes part of the stomach too.

During this period, the board did not disclose to the public his condition, and neither did Steve. He finally accepted the surgery in August 2004, admitting, 'I should have gotten it earlier.' The surgery was successful in the short term, but who knows how he would ultimately have fared if he had followed doctors' advice? He returned to work within just a few weeks.

Meanwhile, as Steve was dealing with his cancer, there was plenty going on around him. All was not well with Disney, for starters. Back in 2003, Steve had fallen out with CEO Michael Eisner. When it came to negotiating a new deal between Disney and Pixar, Steve had specified terms that were extremely bad for Disney, the sole purpose of which appeared to be to force the two companies into parting ways. This duly happened: they separated, and Steve began looking for a new distributor. Later, Disney would push out Eisner and the new CEO, Bob Iger, would take pains to restore the broken relationship.

This was also the time at which Abdulfattah 'John' Jandali found out that Steve was his son. Accounts differ about the amount of contact the two subsequently had. Either way, it was little or none. Steve had no real interest in meeting the man who had abandoned him, his mother and sister. Jandali later sent Steve his medical history to see if there was anything that could help with his own illness, and wrote the occasional brief email with messages of support. He says that he received only two replies, both very short. The second one arrived six weeks before Steve died and said only, 'Thank you.'

Earlier in September 2004, the iMac G5 was unveiled at the Paris Expo. Steve, who had had so much influence in the company and on its products was still recuperating. Instead, Phil Schiller, senior vice president of Worldwide Marketing, presented it. 'It really is a breakthrough in personal computing,' he told the crowd. 'I think that's what Apple is all about.' Arguably, Apple was all about Steve, and he was most conspicuous by his absence. 'He's doing great, and will be back at work in September,' Schiller said. 'September can't come soon enough.'

Knowing that he now had to explain his absence, he finally went public, writing to Apple's employees, briefly telling him of his illness and that he was now 'cured' – despite the fact there was no way he could know that at this stage. Several months later, at the Stanford Commencement Speech in June 2005, he would provide a few more details in a rare window into his private life. 'About a year ago I was diagnosed with cancer. I had a scan at 7:30 in the morning, and it clearly showed a tumor on my pancreas. I didn't even know what a pancreas was. The doctors told me this was almost certainly a type of cancer that is incurable, and that I should expect to live no longer than three to six months. My doctor advised me to go home and get my affairs in order, which is doctor's code for prepare to die. It means to try to tell your kids everything you thought you'd have the next 10 years to tell them in just a few months. It means to make sure everything is buttoned up so that it will be as easy as possible for your family. It means to say your goodbyes.

'I lived with that diagnosis all day. Later that evening I had a biopsy, where they stuck an endoscope down my throat, through my stomach and into my intestines, put a needle into my pancreas and got a few cells from the tumor. I was sedated, but my wife, who was there, told me that when they viewed the cells under a microscope the doctors started crying because it turned out to be a very rare form of pancreatic cancer that is curable with surgery. I had the surgery and I'm fine now.'

It had been nine months between diagnosis and public announcement: nine months in which customers, employees and shareholders were kept in the dark. A lot of the latter were not happy, since Steve's health was ostensibly tied closely to that of Apple's. Legal opinion differed, but generally agreed that Steve had a right to his privacy and therefore wasn't obligated to disclose his condition.

The iMac G5 was the latest in the iMac line and a storming success. AllThings' review gave it the highest praise: nothing could touch it. 'We've been testing this new iMac, and our verdict is that it's the gold standard of desktop PCs. To put it simply: No desktop offered by Dell or Hewlett-Packard or Sony or Gateway can match the new iMac G5's combination of power, elegance, simplicity, ease of use, built-in software, stability and security. From setup to performing the most intense tasks, it's a pleasure to use. And, contrary to common misconceptions, this Mac is competitively priced, when compared with comparably equipped midrange Windows PCs; and it handles all common Windows files, as well as the Internet and email, with aplomb.' In other words, it was Apple all over.

The iMac G5 was outstanding, but it was a computer. The perfect digital hub, perhaps, but still only a computer. Steve had seen a vision of the future a while ago that he was busy bringing about, and in it Apple wasn't a computer company. It was a lifestyle company. He had accelerated this change with the advent of the iPod, and the Apple stores on the high street that analysts had predicted would fail but were wildly successful against all expectations.

The iPhone was the final step in that process, the last piece of the puzzle. The 'i' that had seemed so prescient found its fullest expression here. The project had actually started back in 2003 with the idea of creating a 'convergence' product that would combine a phone, a PDA and an iPod. It took four years to complete.

Along the way, Steve had to swallow another of his former viewpoints. Just as he had considered Microsoft the Enemy before they teamed up on his return to Apple, he despised the big phone networks – which he referred to as 'orifices'. Now that he was looking to create a cellphone, he would have to change his mind about that. And, given his clout, they were only too happy about that. Apple moving into this new area of technology was a huge opportunity for them. Even if it was a shot in the dark and the company was untested, the benefits would be enormous if it paid off. Steve was in a position of considerable strength, and drove a hard bargain. 'We talked to several of them and educated ourselves,' he said, eventually opting for AT&T's Cingular network. 'They were willing to take a really big gamble on us. We decided what the phone is. We decided what software would be on the phone. And so we could make the product we wanted.'

This time, Steve was well enough to unveil the device himself at the Macworld Expo in 2007. It was a two hour-long presentation in front of a rapt audience of 4,000 – some of whom had queued all night to make sure they got a spot. Steven Levy described the ground-breaking and iconic product for the Daily Beast, noting that the three disparate systems of which it comprised were 'superbly integrated. The look of the device is classic Apple: stunningly austere, with a lush 3.5-inch screen ringed in black and a single button underneath. There are also controls (for volume and ring-silencing) on its slim sides (less than half an inch thick), but they are almost imperceptible. The real controls are built into the software – task-appropriate buttons, switches, sliders, and scroll bars that appear on the high-density "multi-touch" screen, which has the intelligence to discern which touches are intentional and which are just random bumps.'

The iPhone was a streak of genius and has impacted the smartphone world more than any other device. It came at a price, naturally – but then, all of Apple's products did. This one would cost either $499 or $599, depending on the amount of memory, and was tied into a two-year contract with Cingular. Customers would often need to purchase more bandwidth for data transfer, too. All in all, it came out as perhaps $200 more than its competitors. But for this, people would pay.

The release of the iPhone was way ahead of its time. Steve knew that it put Apple far in front of the competition. 'This is five years ahead of what everybody else has got,' he said. 'If we didn't do one more thing, we'd be set for five years!' Remember, this was back in 2007, when smartphones were just beginning to take a real hold of the market. Whereas devices like the Blackberry were popular in the business community, smartphones in general and the iPhone in particular had the potential to be so much more – the most powerful lifestyle device ever created to date. 'I see a lot of soccer moms with smart phones,' he said. 'A lot.'

The first iPhone sold over 6 million units over its first 15 months. By the end of 2007, Apple stock hit almost $200 per share, before temporarily falling back over the next few months. The iPhone completed the transition from a computer to a lifestyle company, and they accordingly dropped the word 'computer' from their name. They were now simply 'Apple Inc.'

2008 saw new and even more popular products, including the MacBook Air, an ultrathin laptop, and a faster and cheaper version of the iPhone that outsold the original in two months. But, as if in hideous parody of Apple's ever-slimmer devices, Steve himself was losing weight and attracting concern. His gaunt appearance led to much speculation that the cancer had returned. He released a statement claiming that it was just a 'common bug', but no one really believed it. It didn't help that Bloomberg released his obituary towards the end of the year. Big press agencies always keep obituaries of famous people so that they can update them and publish them quickly in the event of their unexpected death. Steve wasn't dead, but it was a nasty irony that it happened when he was looking so ill. Moreover, other Apple execs were taking the centre stage more and more, with Steve cutting right back on publicity work.

He finally informed the public what was going on five days into 2009, the day before that year's Macworld Expo. His statement was released on Apple's website. 'As many of you know, I have been losing weight throughout 2008. The reason has been a mystery to me and my doctors. A few weeks ago, I decided that getting to the root cause of this and reversing it needed to become my #1 priority. Fortunately, after further testing, my doctors think they have found the cause – a hormone imbalance that has been "robbing" me of the proteins my body needs to be healthy. Sophisticated blood tests have confirmed this diagnosis.' Steve stepped back from the day-to-day running of Apple to allow him to recover, but once again, all was not as it seemed.

It would later come out that Steve received a liver transplant that April. Pancreatic tumours, even the ones that don't prove fatal on the scale of weeks or months, often metastasize, throwing out other tumours into other organs – like the liver. This is what had happened in Steve's case, resulting in liver failure and necessitating a transplant. His sister, Mona Simpson, spoke movingly at his funeral of how he had determinedly picked himself up after that surgery and regained control over his body. 'I remember my brother learning to walk again, with a chair. After his liver transplant, once a day he would get up on legs that seemed too thin to bear him, arms pitched to the chair back. He'd push that chair down the Memphis hospital corridor towards the nursing station and then he'd sit down on the chair, rest, turn around and walk back again. He counted his steps and, each day, pressed a little farther... He tried. He always, always tried, and always with love at the core of that effort. He was an intensely emotional man.'

Mona also stated that she believed he was not fighting to recover for himself, but for his family. 'I realized during that terrifying time that Steve was not enduring the pain for himself. He set destinations: his son Reed's graduation from high school, his daughter Erin's trip to Kyoto, the launching of a boat he was building on which he planned to take his family around the world and where he hoped he and Laurene would someday retire.' It seems that something else about him changed at this point, and he grew more open-minded about charities that he had, previously, had a reputation for spurning. He would start giving large donations and speaking out as an advocate of organ donation, helping to create America's first organ donor registry the next year.

Steve was back at work two months after his transplant, fascinated with the idea of creating a tablet computer. Like so many of Apple's products, this wasn't a new concept – it was just something they would do better than any of their competitors. Perhaps surprisingly, the inception of this most advanced product, the iPad, actually occurred before the iPhone, almost ten years before it was released. 'I actually started on the tablet first. I had this idea of being able to get rid of the keyboard, type on a multitouch glass display,' he later said. 'And I asked our folks, could we come up with a multitouch display – that I could rest my hands on, and actually type on? And about six months later, they called me in and showed me this prototype display. And it was amazing. This is in the early 2000s. And I gave it to one of our other, really brilliant user interface folks, and he called me back a few weeks later and he had inertial scrolling working, and a few other things. Now we were thinking about building a phone at that time, and when I saw the rubber band, inertial scrolling and a few of the other things, I thought "My God, we could build a phone out of this." And I put the tablet project on the shelf, because the phone was more important. And we took the next several years, and did the iPhone.'

If expectations about the iPhone had been high, the iPad was something else. This time, Steve unveiled it himself, sitting on a couch and demonstrating how the device worked during his presentation. The hype had been tremendous, with Steve calling it a 'magical device' with his characteristic – but not, with hindsight, always inaccurate – hyperbole. Analysts didn't agree, deeming it a larger version of the iPod touch. He was vindicated, once again, by Apple's customers, who turned out in their droves to purchase this new tablet computer. Apple sold 7.5 million within nine months.

The iPad was Steve's last gift to Apple, and to its fans. In the 15 years he had been back at the company he had overseen a catalogue of brilliant devices: the iMac, in its several incarnations, iTunes and the iPod, the iPhone and iPad. His health deteriorating further, it was now time to step back for good. Having been on medical leave since January 2011, he finally resigned as CEO in August, though agreed to stay on as Apple's chairman of the board.

Shares in Apple fell five percent in after-hours trading, though analysts said this was comparatively small given how critical Steve had been to the success of the company over the preceding 15 years. Plus, with his health in the news for so long, it was not as big a shock as it might have been.

It was clear to those closest to him that Steve wasn't going to get better now. Steve himself knew this, and he seems to have sought peace with his loved ones as his time drew nearer. 'I know that living with me was not a bowl of cherries,' he told one interviewer.

In her eulogy at his funeral, his sister Mona Simpson spoke movingly of his last days and hours. Of how Steve went through 67 nurses before he found the three he could work with, and to whom he was fiercely loyal from that point on. Of how, suffering from pneumonia and unable to speak, he sketched new devices for the iPad and new hospital equipment.

Of how the entrance of his wife, Laurene, never failed to bring a smile to his face, no matter how great his suffering.

'None of us knows for certain how long we'll be here,' Mona said. 'On Steve's better days, even in the last year, he embarked upon projects and elicited promises from his friends at Apple to finish them. Some boat builders in the Netherlands have a gorgeous stainless steel hull ready to be covered with the finishing wood. His three daughters remain unmarried, his two youngest still girls, and he'd wanted to walk them down the aisle as he'd walked me the day of my wedding.' Though his death was expected, she says, it still came as a shock.

'Tuesday morning, he called me to ask me to hurry up to Palo Alto. His tone was affectionate, dear, loving, but like someone whose luggage was already strapped onto the vehicle, who was already on the beginning of his journey, even as he was sorry, truly deeply sorry, to be leaving us. He started his farewell and I stopped him. I said, "Wait. I'm coming. I'm in a taxi to the airport. I'll be there."

'When I arrived, he and his Laurene were joking together like partners who'd lived and worked together every day of their lives. He looked into his children's eyes as if he couldn't unlock his gaze. Until about two in the afternoon, his wife could rouse him, to talk to his friends from Apple. Then, after awhile, it was clear that he would no longer wake to us. His breathing changed. It became severe, deliberate, purposeful. I could feel him counting his steps again, pushing farther than before. This is what I learned: he was working at this, too. Death didn't happen to Steve, he achieved it.

'Steve's final words, hours earlier, were monosyllables, repeated three times. Before embarking, he'd looked at his sister

Patti, then for a long time at his children, then at his life's partner, Laurene, and then over their shoulders past them. Steve's final words were: OH WOW. OH WOW. OH WOW.'

'What I learned from my brother's death was that character is essential: What he was, was how he died. We all – in the end – die in medias res,' Mona said. 'In the middle of a story. Of many stories.'

Epilogue:
legacy of a genius

At Steve's Stanford Commencement Address, which
he gave in the period after his initial recovery from
cancer, he said the following. 'Almost everything
– all external expectations, all pride, all fear of
embarrassment or failure – these things just fall away in
the face of death, leaving only what is truly important.
Remembering that you are going to die is the best
way I know to avoid the trap of thinking you have
something to lose. You are already naked. There is
no reason not to follow your heart.' Steve's heart was
for beauty, and Apple are going to have a hard time
replacing his consuming passion for what he did.

Speaking to the Australian Broadcast Network, Jeffrey
Young argued that the company would be profoundly
affected by Steve's death. He was, after all, the man
who had co-founded the company and who had driven
it on, for good or bad, for almost 25 years. Even his
absence in the late 1980s and early 1990s had shaped
the company. His guiding hand simply can't be replaced.

'I think that you're going to see a change in Apple. Much of Apple's success is because of an emotional reaction that many people have with Steve and with his products. He's really a remarkable human being and somebody who transcends the technology space. And because of that people feel a real connection to Apple that I think is going to dissipate with time.

'Also, Apple's going to be very hard pressed to produce the kind of products and the excitement that they have when there's Steve. Steve is a unique guy. He's a perfectionist and a driven perfectionist who really has a confidence in his own talent that no-one else could have. He's had 30 years at the pinnacle of the technology industry. He's changed many industries and that is just unheard of anywhere else and so I just don't think you can replace that in any kind of short term sense.'

Apple consequently faces a series of major challenges. Steve's legacy will last for some time – as he said, the iPhone and other products put them several years ahead of the competition. But that head start won't last forever. Apple's best-selling devices – the iPhone, iPod and iPad, as well as the iTunes store – will carry them through for a while. But without the vision of someone like Steve, it could be like the 1980s again, when the Apple II kept the company afloat as they struggled to come up with the Mac that would put an end to their survival on borrowed time. Then again, in the early 90s, the Mac would be the product on which they still relied as a series of failures stymied their options for the future. Apple's execs and its new CEO cannot allow that to happen. 'I think Apple's big problems are going to be in the sort of mid-term, the next five years. I think Apple right now has a very good product line. It's going to do very well. Steve set them up very well and but going forward they're going to have a hard time replicating that, continuing to succeed like that.'

Exactly how Apple far over the medium term has yet to be seen. But Steve's legacy is far wider than for Apple alone. The developments he oversaw over the last 30 years or more have had industry-wide and world-wide ramifications.

Just one of the ways in which he hoped Apple would transform the world was in the field of education. Apple has always had links with schools and colleges, recognising them as a huge potential market. Steve had discussed with Barack Obama and Bill Gates the way that technology should be able to change education. Lectures could be shifted to students' own time, watched on iPads or other computers; that way, classes could be devoted to discussion and group problem-solving. Plus, the computer had the ability to totally change the way textbooks worked, turning them from blocks of text into interactive lessons. 'The process by which states certify textbooks is corrupt,' he once said. 'But if we can make the textbook free, and they come with the iPad... we can give them an opportunity to circumvent the whole process and save money.'

Fans and analysts of Steve and his work have had trouble finding a figure with which to compare him, someone who has had the same extent and nature of impact he has. There are many contenders, but none seem to fit perfectly. Some have suggested Leonardo da Vinci as a visionary who was far ahead of his time, but da Vinci was an inventor and artist. Steve was an entrepreneur – a visionary, certainly, but someone who spurred others on to great work. Others in the Apple team may have had the technical expertise to make the products, but he had the inspiration and charisma to encourage them to do so.

Andy Hertzfeld, who worked with Steve on the Macintosh in the early 80s, suggested to Top Spot that 'Since Steve was primarily a businessman who worked with teams to revolutionize many industries, I think Edison is an apt comparison. Da Vinci isn't a good comparison, since he wasn't a businessman and was more of a solo act.'

Jeffrey Young accepted the comparison, but qualified it by saying that 'Edison... was an extraordinary inventor as well. So I'm not sure you know they're correspondent. The person that I think is the closest to Steve in history, in the history of modern business, is Howard Hughes.' Hughes, the character played by Leonardo di Caprio in the movie The Aviator, was a business magnate whose interests spanned everything from film to aviation engineering. Having made his mark in Hollywood as a producer and director of a number of high-profile films, he moved into aviation, catalysing the industry into making fast, reliable air travel affordable for the masses. 'The difference between them was that Steve was born as an orphan and was raised by a blue collar family in the Bay area. His dad was a machinist. Howard Hughes' family owned a machine tool company in Texas and Howard Hughes was born rich. He was always rich. But in the breadth of the products that Howard Hughes produced, I think he's the only person who is close to Steve. Steve has made enormous contributions to the music industry, to the computer industry, to the movie industry and animation industries. I think you can argue that Hughes with his helicopters and his movie innovations had a similar breadth of influence.'

Steve's legacy is by no means complete. The way in which he helped revolutionise personal computing has had, and will continue to have, far-reaching consequences. Apple's products transformed the way business is done, the way we interact with each other, the way our lives are lived. They have had a profound effect on culture, and it is no exaggeration to say that they have and will continue to reverberate across every area of our existences. The changes that his products have brought about in our world will never be undone. They have shaped not only our work and personal lives, the way we communicate and relate to one another, but the very fabric of our society.